Excel

BASIC SKILLS

AGES 10 to 12

CREATIVE WRITING

YEARS 5–6

Get the Results You Want!

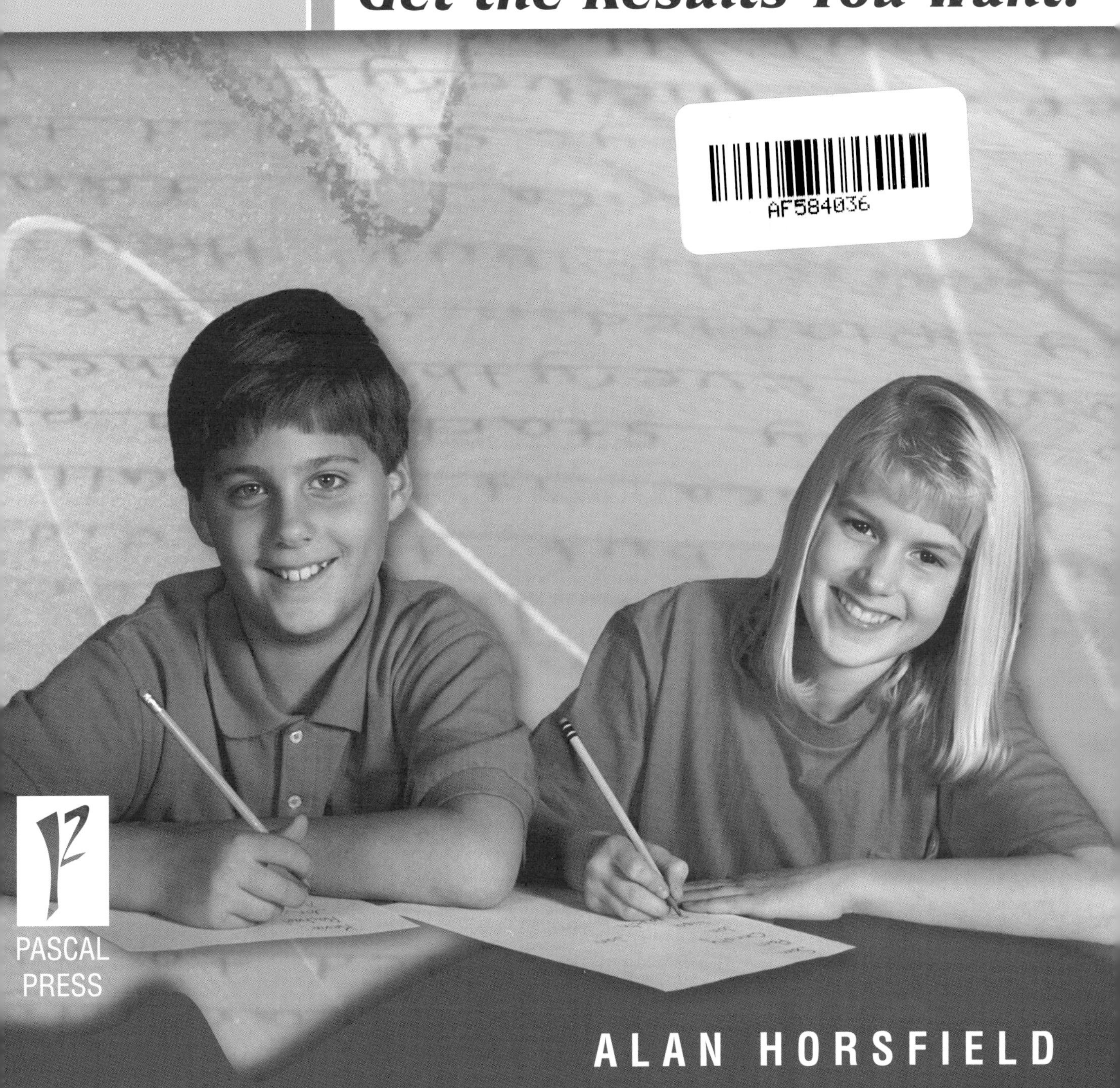

PASCAL PRESS

ALAN HORSFIELD

... one can argue that there is a basic human need for narrative: it is one of the fundamental tools for making sense of experience – has been, back as far as you can go in history.

From *Thinks ...* by David Lodge, Penguin Books, London, 2002

Reprinted 2005, 2008 (twice), 2009, 2011

Updated in 2013 for the Australian Curriculum

Reprinted 2015, 2017, 2018, 2020, 2022

ISBN 978 1 74125 082 4

Pascal Press
PO Box 250
Glebe NSW 2037
(02) 8585 4050
www.pascalpress.com.au

Publisher: Vivienne Joannou
Project Editor: Grant Bailey
Edited by Christine Eslick
Australian Curriculum updates edited by Frances Wade
Page design and typesetting by Larissa Petryca (ID360)
Additional typesetting by Leanne Richters (Grizzly Graphics)
Cover by DiZign Pty Ltd
Printed by Vivar Printing/Green Giant Press

Table of Contents

About the author

Alan Horsfield taught for many years in schools across New South Wales. In 1980 he went to Papua New Guinea as principal of an international school. In the early 1990s he returned to Australia to resume teaching in the eastern suburbs of Sydney.

On leaving teaching he began to write children's textbooks and children's stories.

In 1994 he became president of the NSW Children's Book Council. He has been a judge for the NSW Premier's Book Awards and spent several years working at the University of New South Wales as an English Research Officer, where he was part of a team constructing assessment tests for schools.

He is now a freelance writer focusing on educational publications for parents and schools. He also provides testing material for assessment organisations and runs writing workshops for primary and secondary students across Australia and New Zealand. Alan has written, co-written or been involved in the writing of over 100 books, including textbooks, educational texts and children's fiction. He has been published in Australia and overseas and has won prizes for his writing in national competitions.

Fiction by Alan Horsfield

So Much for Aliens, Thomson Learning Australia, 1996
The Big Race, Thomson Learning Australia, 1997
'Lemming Run' in *Then and Now*, Wannabee Publishing, 1997
The Ghost Writer, Macmillan Educational, Crackers series, 1997
Monopillar, Thomson Learning Australia, 1997
Bubble Buster, Blake Education, Sparklers series, 1998
The Aitutaki Phantom, Thomson Learning Australia, 1999 (set in the Cook Islands)
My Sad Skeleton, Wendy Pye NZ, Galaxy Kids series, 2002
The Strange World of Elmer Floyd, Longman Pearson, Just Kids series, 2002
Daily Bread, Blake Education, Gigglers series, 2002
'Dream on, Brian' in *Dreams*, Ginninderra Press, 2002 (children's stories collection)
The Brahmin and the Ungrateful Tiger, Nelson ITP, 2003
The Rats of Wolfe Island, Lothian, 2002 (young adult fiction set in Fiji)
Dr awKwarD, Macmillan NZ, 2003
Cadaver Dog, Lothian, Crime Waves mystery, 2003
Great Hair Robbery, Lothian, 2003
Why the Turtle Does Not Fly, Macmillan Education, 2005
Clumsy Clinton, Macmillan Springboard, 2005
The Frightened Scarecrow, Macmillan Springboard, 2005
Uncanny Climate Change, Macmillan Springboard, 2007
T C Ami, Macmillan Future Scientists, 2007
The Toilet Paper Rip Off, Aussie! Aussie! Aussie! 2008
Life at Sea, Macmillan Literacy Network, 2009

Extracts from a number of the above books and stories have been used in this guide.

Acknowledgements

Material from the following works have been quoted in the book:

Cadaver Dog, Alan Horsfield, Lothian Books, 2003

Daily Bread, Alan Horsfield, Blake Education, Sydney, 2002

Freddie the Frightened, Pamela Shrapnel, Angus & Robertson, 1988

Holly and the Frog Prince, Elaine Horsfield, Learning Media Ltd, NZ, 1999

Monopillar, Alan Horsfield, Thomson Learning Australia, Australia, 1998

Night of the Muttonbirds, Mary Small, HBJ Spectrum, 1992

Sit down, Mum, there's something I've got to tell you, Moya Simons, Penguin Group Australia, 1995

Spooked, Errol Broome, HBJ Spectrum, 1992

'Streetscape', Ian Steep, from *Through the Web and Other Stories,* HBJ Spectrum, 1992

Talking in Whispers, James Watson, Fontana Lions, 1985

The Aitutaki Phantom, Alan Horsfield, Thomson Learning Australia, 2000

The Big Race, Alan Horsfield, Thomson Learning Australia, 1997

The Fat and Juicy Place, Diana Kidd, Angus and Robertson (Griffin Paperbacks), Adelaide SA, 1992

The Ghost Writer, Alan Horsfield, Macmillan Education Australia, 1997

The Rats of Wolfe Island, Alan Horsfield, Lothian Books, 2002

The Strange World of Elmer Floyd, Alan Horsfield, Longman Pearson, 2002

The Sylvia Mystery, Penny Hall, HBJ Spectrum, 1992

Unreal, Paul Jennings, Penguin Group Australia, 1985

White Sheep, poet/source not known

'Zeppo', Virginia King, from *Through the Web and Other Stories*, HBJ Spectrum, 1992

Many thanks to Elaine Horsfield (EJH Talent Promotion P/L) for support, proofreading and valued criticism. Thanks, too, to Val Andrews and the students of Domremy College, Five Dock, who have participated in a number of workshops and provided valued feedback for this book.

To the student

This book is not intended to teach you about correct punctuation, parts of speech or grammar, spelling or types of texts. That is all done in class by your classroom teacher. This book is a practical guide to writing fiction (narratives and stories). It presents the various skills required to write better fiction, showing you ways to make your writing more appealing and more interesting.

The different writing skills are introduced in turn, with some explanation or a quick revision of the practical knowledge you will need to implement the skill. Wherever practical, extracts from published stories have been included to show you 'how it has been done'. There are also exercises so that you can practise what you have learnt. The answers given for writing tasks are suggested responses only.

Improvements in your writing won't occur simply by reading the book. Like all skills these have to be practised. Netball players or cricketers don't just know the rules and develop an understanding of how to play the game, they get out there and practise. Just as with any skill the more you practise the better you become. Runners run nearly every day. Serious writers write nearly every day.

The biggest problem in writing is **procrastination**–putting off getting started. The only way to defeat procrastination is actually to start writing. The first few words or sentences may seem false or lack planning or even be corny, but once most people start writing the words begin to flow with greater ease. Think of a runner starting to train. The first few paces may be hard, but once the runner has developed a rhythm it becomes easier.

Two other words of advice. First, don't be afraid to let other people read your stories. Stories are meant for an audience, and this may include publication. When you are aware that others will be reading, or listening, to your creative efforts you become more critical of the words you use and the way your story unfolds. It keeps you on your toes, so to speak. Reading stories aloud to an audience (even an audience of one!) gives you a chance to make corrections, amendments and improvements to your work.

Second, remember to treat your readers as intelligent, imaginative people who also have had experience that they will bring to your writing. Don't try to spoonfeed them. Let them use their imagination and experiences when reading your stories. There is a chapter in the book that helps you do this (Chapter 20: Showing, not telling).

Write with passion and let your imagination run free!

Writing narratives

What is a **narrative**? It is a way of telling a story. The story might be a fable or fantasy. It might be historical or imagined.

A narrative is **not a recount**. The main purpose of a recount is to retell past events or experiences. Recounts usually retell events in the order they happened.

Narratives do more than retelling a series of events. They try to create experiences that are shared with the reader. The writer uses many literary techniques to capture the reader's attention. This book will introduce you to some of these techniques.

(answer page 114)

Read these two extracts and decide which is a recount and which is a narrative. Write your choice in the space underneath each extract.

Extract 1

Bella, the Getz family cat, disappeared for three days. Each day, one of the family members would take a walk around the nearby streets softly calling her name. It seemed as if she had finally left home.

Then, late on the third day, she returned. Her paws were sore and her coat didn't have that licked-clean look. Although the family was excited with Bella's return, Bella was quite indifferent. She checked out her food bowl, which had been filled to overflowing. Then she wandered over to her cushion on the old plastic chair and sniffed it. Then she hopped up onto it and found a cosy place to go to sleep.

Extract 2

Saturday she disappeared.

On Sunday Marcia trudged around the nearby streets calling her name to no avail. Marcia would have spent the whole day searching the streets but her father said no cat was worth that much effort.

Before work on Monday, Mr Getz took a brisk walk around the block. No cat.

Tuesday morning, and Mrs Getz explored several of the nearby blocks. Still no cat.

It was a sad family that made silent preparations for the evening meal. Then, without warning, Bella strolled in!

The first extract was a recount and the second was a narrative (part of a story). Read the two opening sentences again. Notice that in the narrative the first sentence attempts to entice the reader to find out just who has disappeared.

Recount (Extract 1): Retells past experiences and events in a factual way
Narrative (Extract 2): Creates a word picture of the situation

Exercise 2

(answer page 114)

From the narrative extract (Extract 2) select five words the writer used to make the writing more vivid and appealing.

__________ __________ __________ __________ __________

Reading and writing task

Read this short recount and rewrite the beginning as a narrative. Remember to use words imaginatively.

It was a fine morning when the small children set off to hike from Planet Rock to Bunyip Pond, a distance of about eight kilometres. Their leader was Leonard Hurst. At first the going was easy as the small group followed him up the ridge. At the end of the ridge they had the choice of going straight down the steep rocky ridge spine or winding their way back and forth across the ridge.

Leonard decided it would be quicker to go straight down. This meant hanging on to trees and rocks as they moved from one level to the next. In some places they had to slide on their backsides before coming to rest against a boulder.

____

____

____

____

____

____

____

Recounts

Recounts are usually in **past tense** (time) whereas the writer of a narrative has more flexibility in use of tense.

Name one recount you have read (or know about).

Narratives

- ➞ Narratives usually use **direct speech** (what is actually said appears in inverted commas) whereas recounts make greater use of indirect speech (e.g. Tom said that he thought the wind would change.)
- ➞ Narratives do not always use complete sentences. Words and phrases are used for impact.
- ➞ Narratives contain facts, descriptions and **atmosphere**. (Atmosphere is the 'feeling' a story creates in the reader's mind/imagination.)

List two narratives that you have read in the last six months.

1. ______________________________

2. ______________________________

Reading task

(answer page 114)

Read the extract below. Highlight any of the narrative features mentioned above. List three of the features you found below the extract.

> Two o'clock. And still no sign of Andy.
>
> Wendy sat on the bus shelter seat looking into the inky blackness of the night. She could hardly distinguish any features in the scrub on the other side of the lonely road, just a few branches that looked like naked arms reaching out from the emptiness of night. And silence.
>
> Then in the darkness across the road a light flashed on and off. She almost missed it and then thought it was a trick the night was playing on her straining eyes.
>
> Then there was a quick double flash. It was not her imagination.
>
> Someone had to be nearby.

1. ______________________________ 2. ______________________________

3. ______________________________

Writing task

Using narrative style, write a few sentences of your own about someone waiting for a bus.

____

____

____

Recognising where ideas for stories come from

Writers on school visits are often asked where they get their ideas for stories. There is no easy answer to this question. There is no secret either.

Once you start writing with enthusiasm, and you want to keep writing, ideas will pop up everywhere. They come at the most unexpected times. That is why many writers carry a small notepad and pen with them wherever they go. I even have pen and paper beside the bed.

Ideas will pop out of:

- → TV shows
- → things that happen in the family
- → things that happen at school
- → other people's books and stories
- → newspapers and magazine articles
- → conversations and chance remarks.

The idea for a story may be a simple incident but the writer sees in it the possibility for a story. The incident grabs the writer's imagination. This does not mean that the writer rushes to his/her office and starts furiously typing a complete story.

Most likely, the idea sits in the writer's imagination and bits of the story start falling into place – the setting, the character, the plot, the detail, the ending. Some writers liken the process to a seed in the garden. There are many seeds in our gardens. Some will be flowers, others will be weeds and some won't germinate at all.

Ideas for my stories

The idea for my story *The Big Race* came from a school sports day, as I watched the kids in a mini-marathon. I knew what must have been going through their minds as I had just competed in the Sydney City to Surf Fun Run.

I didn't write the story until much later. But the idea was there all the time – not always at the front of my mind but certainly in my little ideas notebook.

The idea for *Cadaver Dog* came to me at an international airport as I watched 'sniffer' dogs check the passengers' luggage. I didn't use the airport as my setting, but rather a combination of schools I had once taught in. I wrote the story many years later.

Writing tip

Keep an ideas notebook for story ideas. The ideas won't always turn into stories but they are there in black and white if you ever get the urge and inspiration to develop them.

On the next page there are spaces for you to jot down ideas as you find them.

Exercise 1

Write down one or two exciting story ideas you have had recently.

Writing tip

From ideas come plots. Don't discard your ideas too readily. One day, in some flash of inspiration, you might just have a prize-winning story.

My ideas notebook

My ideas notebook has over fifty story ideas – most of which I may never use. However, I find it comforting to have written down the ideas and know I won't forget them. Sometimes an idea seems fantastic to begin with and then the more I think about it the more difficult (or silly) it seems.

Here are a few ideas from my notebook. I have no ideas about the characters or the plots for these stories. It's just that at one time I liked the ideas.

1. Hidden mobile phone found ringing near a bank.
2. A tattoo that comes to life.
3. Clockwork mice versus battery-driven mice war.
4. A pink (or another colour) snowman.
5. Visitors from another planet capture earthlings to be slaves back home.

As you can see, the ideas are quite unusual but there is a germ of an idea there that may be developed at a later date.

Exercise 2

Quickly jot down some ideas the following graphics might suggest for stories.

1. ______

2. ______

3. ______________________________

____

Writing task

On this page start your own list of story ideas. Don't worry if they sound different from other ideas mentioned in this chapter.

1. ______________________________
2. ______________________________
3. ______________________________
4. ______________________________
5. ______________________________
6. ______________________________
7. ______________________________
8. ______________________________
9. ______________________________
10. ______________________________

If you find you have many exciting ideas get your own special ideas notebook.

Writing what you know - first-hand experiences

Many good stories draw heavily on the experiences of the writer. A story you write about an event in your home, street or town will have a more authentic note to it than, say, a story set in Moscow or Miami if you have never been there.

One of my more successful books (*The Rats of Wolfe Island*) was set in Fiji – just down the road from where I lived. I could check out the 'concrete' detail regularly. No doubt, to readers in Alice Springs or Arizona, the setting is fascinating. To me it's rather ordinary. I have had stories set in the Cook Islands, outback New South Wales, the inner suburbs of Sydney – and they are all places where I have lived or worked.

Don't be embarrassed by the fact that your setting seems ordinary. If the story is well written then the setting will be interesting to the reader. It's most likely the reader doesn't know your setting so it will be new to that reader.

Writing tip
Write about real life experiences. Write about what is happening in your real world.

Experience counts

Many recognised writers are 'older' people. They have had a variety of life experiences. It can be difficult to write about love, death, loneliness and rejection if you have never experienced them.

Older people can, however, get out of touch with what's happening in the real world of younger people. Many published first novels were written when the authors were teenagers.

Make a list of settings you could write about with some confidence (e.g. shopping mall, holiday place).

______________________ ______________________

______________________ ______________________

______________________ ______________________

Exercise 2

Make a list of experiences that you could write about with some confidence (e.g. winning or losing a sporting match, being home alone, getting lost).

____________________ ____________________ ____________________

____________________ ____________________ ____________________

____________________ ____________________ ____________________

Exercise 3

(answer page 114)

Make a list of feelings that you could write about with some confidence (e.g. excitement, disappointment, frustration).

____________________ ____________________ ____________________

____________________ ____________________ ____________________

Exercise 4

(answer page 114)

Make a list of characters that you could write about with some confidence (e.g. bully, grandparent, enthusiastic teacher).

______________________________ ______________________________

______________________________ ______________________________

______________________________ ______________________________

First-hand and secondary experiences

There are two types of experiences you can draw on when writing.

1. **First-hand experiences** are things that have happened to you. If, as a writer, you want to write about someone at a police station, *you* should go to a police station. My basic setting for the story *Monopillar* was the Sydney Monorail. I did several circuits on the Sydney Monorail, taking notes. I went after the first-hand experience I needed.
2. However, because of the subject matter, it is sometimes difficult or even impossible to have a first-hand experience. You have to rely on **secondary experiences**, on information from other sources. Information is available from many sources. For *Ghost Writer* I had to know something

about voodoo. I went to the local library and looked up books on voodoo. I used someone else's experiences and knowledge (secondary experiences).

Exercise 5 **(answer page 114)**

List some places you may be able to find useful information for a story you want to research.

______________________________ ______________________________

______________________________ ______________________________

Writing tip

Don't overlook your parents (and grandparents) as good secondary sources. Start at home and with all those you are familiar with.

Always check your sources

Take care with information from any source. If you are not sure of the difference between, say, a turtle and a tortoise and you don't bother to check it out you can bet your life some of your readers will know the difference and, for them, your story will be 'full of holes'. It will lack authenticity.

Don't use words you aren't fully sure of and hope that the readers will forgive you for your ignorance. They won't!

Exercise 6 **(answer page 114)**

What *is* the difference between a turtle and a tortoise?

____

____

Research **(answer page 114)**

Following are five statements. Tick ✓ the ones that are correct and cross ✗ the ones that contain incorrect information.

1. The Amazon River is the longest river in the world.
2. Ronald Reagan acted in cowboy films before becoming president of the United States of America.
3. The story *The Hare and the Tortoise* was first told two thousand years ago.

4. Origami is a form of Japanese self-defence.
5. The author of *The Wind in the Willows* is the Englishman Kenneth Grahame.

Here are four topics: bungy jumping, solar flares, poison ivy, Captain Thunderbolt.

Choose one of the topics to research, and then write a short **narrative** piece using that information. (There may only be enough room to start your writing. You can continue on a separate piece of paper.)

Choosing titles (What's in a name?)

The title of a story is very important. The title:

- suggests the subject matter of the story
- suggests the kind of story
- gives a clue to the tone or style of writing
- may even suggest the age group of the reader.

For example, consider *The Cabbage Patch Fib* by Paul Jennings. This title suggests:

Subject: Where babies come from (under cabbages?)

Kind of story: Family situation

Tone or style: Amusing, humorous

Age group: Younger readers

Exercise 1

(answer page 114)

There's a book in the school library, *Death on the High Trapeze.* What does the title suggest to you?

Subject: ______________________________

Kind of story: ______________________________

Tone or style: ______________________________

Age group: ______________________________

There are times when you have to read part of the story before the reason for the title becomes obvious (e.g. *Minnie* by Annie M.G. Schmidt).

Exercise 2

For many school exercises the teacher provides the title. In 'free choice' writing or even writing for a competition you may be required to provide your own title. Many competitions just give a general theme. In one competition for children's stories the theme was 'Dreams'. My entry was titled 'Dream on, Brian!'

What suggestion do you have for an entry? ______________________________

Writing task 1

(answer page 114)

What age group do you think a story with the title 'Pirate Pam's Purple Parrot' is suitable for?

____

Write a few sentences about the parrot.

____

____

____

Writing tip

Many writers can't begin writing until they have a title. My suggestion is to start writing and worry about the title later. Sometimes it suddenly jumps out at you. In one of my earlier stories the title was the last line of the story: 'So Much for Aliens!' It is best if the title can entice the reader to find out more about your story.

Techniques for creating titles

Single word titles
Moonstorm (Kim Wilkins)
Monopillar (A. Horsfield)
Dingo
Stranded (Jan Thorburn)
Blubber (Judy Blume)

Exclamation titles
What a Goat! (Errol Broome)
Relax Max! (Brian Caswell)
Lookout!
Surprise Attack!
Titans! (M. Stephens)

Unusual mixtures
The Green Wind (T. Fowler)
Skating on Sand (Libby Gleeson)
Stone Baby (Beth Norling)
Man Bites Dog (Adam Ford)

Descriptions
The Girl from Glenrock
The Rats of Wolfe Island (A. Horsfield)
The Secret Beach (Jackie French)
Treasure Island (R.L. Stevenson)

Alliteration
Monster Man (Glyn Parry)
Bubble Buster (A. Horsfield)
My Sad Skeleton (A. Horsfield)
Chadwick's Chimney (Colin Thiele)

Rhymes
A Horse of Course (Margaret Clark)
Frank's Pranks
Cat in the Hat (P.D. Eastman)
Staying Alive in Year Five (John Marsden)

Contrasts
Beggars' Bank
Summer Snow
My Worst Best Friend (Max Dann)
Frozen Fire (James Houston)

Puns (word plays)
Sherlock Bones (Con Brecon)
A Grave Business (A. Horsfield)
Slay Ride
Dead on Time

Questions
Who Stole the Tarts?
What About Tomorrow? (Ivan Southall)
What Did Simon Say?

Amusing titles

Unreal Banana Peel (June Factor)

The Cabbage Patch Fib (Paul Jennings)

Teasers

Sit down, Mum, there's something I've got to tell you (Moya Simons)

The Best Kept Secret (Emily Rodda)

Two of my favourites

Dreamslip (Brian Caswell)

Dear Nobody (Berlie Doherty)

Exercise 3

(answer page 114)

List four real titles you thought were clever or appropriate.

1. ______________________________

2. ______________________________

3. ______________________________

4. ______________________________

Exercise 4

Create titles for these children's stories. Use some of the techniques listed above.

Two girls lost on Mt Everest in a snowstorm ______________________________

An alien mouse joins a family of kitchen mice ______________________________

A car race across a desert ______________________________

A zebra without stripes ______________________________

A body is discovered in a flower garden ______________________________

A telephone that answers back ______________________________

Now create some titles of your own.

Single word titles: ____________________

Exclamation titles: ____________________

Unusual mixtures: ____________________

Descriptions: ____________________

Alliteration: ____________________

Rhymes: ____________________

Contrasts: ____________________

Puns (word plays): ____________________

Questions: ____________________

Amusing titles: ____________________

Teasers: ____________________

Writing tip

Keep a list in your **ideas notebook** of titles you like or have created. It is so easy to forget ideas if you don't write them down. Start a temporary collection here.

5 Knowing the importance of detail—concrete or general

Using concrete detail can lift a piece of story writing from the ordinary to the visually exciting.

Reading task 1

Compare these three paragraphs to see what differences the detail makes.

1. Brett drove his car along the road to the beach. He felt happy. Soon he would be at the beach and ready for the surf. He grabbed some food from the adjacent seat and began to eat it.
2. Brett drove his Ford wagon along the track to the beach house. He whistled a catchy tune. Soon he would be at the clubhouse and ready for the surf. He grabbed an apple from the adjacent seat and began to munch it.
3. Brett gunned his red Mustang along Highway 21 to the beach resort. He sang along with his latest CD. Soon he would be at Bell Beach and ready for the waves. He selected a salad roll from the adjacent leather seat and took a small bite.

When you read each extract you see a different boy going to the beach, although all three are doing much the same thing. Nothing is actually said about the boys' characters but the detail gives an indication of their lifestyles. Details bring the last two extracts alive in your mind.

Exercise 1

(answer page 114)

Give a specific example for these general terms. The first is done for you.

vehicle	utility	TV show	________
tree	________	flower	________
jam	________	film	________
drink	________	fish	________
house	________	ball	________
magazine	________	neighbour	________

Detail gives insight to character or action

As you can see, specific details give more than just facts to your writing. They give an insight into the character or action. This applies not only to nouns but also to other parts of speech (adjectives, adverbs, verbs and so on). Compare these sets of sentences.

1. Gerry held the reins of the horse in her hand.
   Gerry held the reins of the black stallion tightly in her sweating hand.
2. Holly's mother read her a story.
   Although she was tired, Holly's mother softly read her favourite fairytale to her.

(answer page 114)

Rewrite these sentences using concrete detail.

1. The cat sat on the mat. ______________________________

2. Paul took the magazine from the rack to the counter. ______________________________

____

Keep detail consistent

Make sure that concrete detail is consistent with the character or setting. Below is a rewrite of the short narrative about Brett from the previous page. Read the passage and note how unrealistic the changes are.

> Brett bounced the vintage car along the rough track to the beach shack. He hummed a sweet tune. Soon he would be at the shack and ready for the surf. He selected a hot meat pie from the adjacent seat and began to chomp on it.

Warning!
When in doubt about specific details, it is wiser to use general terms than to make mistakes.

The concrete detail in the following extract gives the reader a sense of the difficulties the men faced setting up camp.

> They made a number of trips ashore in the dinghy, Big Tom pulling at the oars and the boat piled high with boxes and bundles containing food for the weekend and the necessary materials for patching and repairing the sheds. Then, when all ashore, they lent their strength to the dinghy, pulling it high up the beach for it was not yet full tide. After dragging the timber and metal drums

up to the line of teatree they shouldered the boxes and bundles and walked to the sheds in silence. A key in a lock, a kick from a boot and the door swung open protesting on its rusty hinges.

From: **Night of the Muttonbirds** by Mary Small

Exercise 2

(answer page 114)

In the above extract the author, Mary Small, could have used general terms in a number of places, for example **scrub** instead of **teatree**.

What words has Mary Small used instead of these words/terms?

1. boat ____________________
2. supplies ____________________
3. carried ____________________
4. pulling ____________________

Writing task 2

(answer page 114)

Rewrite the following incidences and situations with as much concrete detail as possible. Each example may be expanded into more than one sentence.

1. The students reacted to the visitor's performance with admiration.

____

____

2. Flies were crawling all over the food set out for their lunch.

____

____

3. She ate the sauce covered pie and washed it down with a soft drink.

____

____

4. The stock roamed over the hills looking for food.

____

____

5. The wind and rain lashed the building for many hours.

6. There was the sound of a tank in the town and the residents hurried indoors.

7. A man stopped by the headstone and read the inscription.

8. As soon as the band started playing their first number the audience joined in.

Creating opening paragraphs that capture the reader's interest

Paragraphs can be from one word to several sentences long. The opening paragraph is important. Apart from the title, it is the first impression the reader gets of your story. It has to grab the reader's attention and make the reader want to find out more. Don't reveal too much, however. The opening paragraph should either intrigue the reader or put questions in the reader's mind: Who is this person? What is happening?

Reading task 1

Read this opening paragraph.

> The email was puzzling. No, it was confusing.
>
> I took it from the pocket of my denim jacket and re-read the terrible typing. It was more than just the typing, it looked as if it had been written by someone not fully coherent, or as if it had been badly copied.

From: **The Rats of Wolfe Island**

What questions does this paragraph give rise to? Here are some that might come to mind:

Why is the email puzzling?

Who is reading the email?

Who wrote the email?

Why is the typing so terrible?

There are no immediate answers. The only way to find out is to read on.

Exercise 1

(answer page 115)

Read the opening paragraph from *The Ghost Writer*. Write down three questions that it suggests and that may make a reader want to find out more.

> He came across the ad by accident. He didn't know why he was even looking at the pathetic magazine. They have the weirdest reading matter in some reception areas. Whoever was in charge put out anything they could lay their hands on. The magazines were more boring than the waiting. Some looked older than he was. They could all be trashed. Still, the ad was intriguing.

From: **The Ghost Writer**

1. ____

2. ____

3. ____

Using speech

Speech, especially starting in the middle of a conversation, can be a good beginning. For example:

> 'You can't be serious,' cried Cindy.
>
> Craig took a deep breath then said, 'Can't see any other way around it.'
>
> 'Have you seen the size of it!' exclaimed Cindy.

Exercise 2

(answer page 115)

When you read the extract above, what questions are already surfacing in your mind? List two of your questions here.

1. ____

2. ____

To find out answers to your questions you would have to read on.

Using unusual words

A striking first sentence with an unusual word or two can also be effective. For example:

> The waif-like child with her limpid eyes stood at the boom gate silently watching the heavily armed guard.

List any words with meaning you are unsure of.

____

Using excitement

Some writers like to start with an exciting or thrilling moment in their story. For example:

> The engine spluttered momentarily.
>
> Alex's heart missed a beat but by the time he had fiddled with the controls the engine had returned to its normal steady drone. He checked the Cessna's instrument panel. Not a lot of fuel. But more than enough to reach the strip. He relaxed.
>
> Suddenly the engine coughed violently and stopped. Warning lights flashed angrily.

Exercise 3

(answer page 115)

With a highlighter, strike out all the unnecessary words or phrases in the short paragraph over the page so that no less information is revealed. (The first one is done for you.)

It was **one of** the most embarrassing moment**s** of my whole life when I won the set of pink baby's clothes in the school raffle. And I don't even like girls, big or little. And what did my friend Kevin do? Laugh, then rush off to tell all the boys in the soccer team.

There are usually fifteen boys who turn up to soccer training. Today twenty-five turned up, including Mad Mike McMahon.

Reading task 2

Here are three examples of opening paragraphs that arouse interest.

There was an eerie silence in the street as Joanne walked home from school. Puzzled, she looked around. Everything seemed normal. Some kids were chasing each other up ahead, and a truck rumbled noisily along the road. Just an ordinary afternoon, so why did everything seem stiller than usual?

From: 'Zeppo' by Virginia King

Michael woke up with a start. Someone was banging on the front door. Heavy footsteps clomped over the bare boards of the hallway. A shouting of voices, Jacko's familiar growl, then the front door slammed shut. Michael shivered and pulled the thin blanket closer around his shoulders. Through the cracked glass of the curtainless window, the sky looked grey and dirty.

From: 'Streetscape' by Ian Steep

Everyone one in Dorking Street knew there was a spook in Gerry's attic wardrobe. Gerry told them all. 'Don't stay the night if you're scared of spooks,' he would say the first time anyone came to stay. And the first time was always the last.

From: **Spooked** by Errol Broome

Exercise 4

Look at some of your recent creative writing with which you feel reasonably happy.

Story titles: ______________________________

Answer these questions:

Is there too much information in the opening paragraph(s)? ______________________

Can some of the information be revealed later in the story? ______________________

Can any words be removed without destroying the meaning or sense? ______________

How well does the opening relate to the rest of the story? ______________________

Does it make you want to read on and find out more? ______________________

Write down one or two ways that you could improve the opening of your story.

Now rewrite the opening paragraph (or first few sentences) of one of a your stories.

7 Choosing closing paragraphs

The closing paragraph(s) should tie up most of the important threads of your story. The reader should feel satisfied that the ordeals your character(s) has been through have been resolved. It doesn't always have to be a happy ending.

Reflecting the first paragraphs

It is often a clever move to have the last few paragraphs reflect the first few paragraphs. This gives the story a rounded-off feeling. In a book that began with an email (see page 19), this is the second last paragraph.

> I touched the pocket of my denim jacket. The email that had brought me on this third and final trip was still there. It didn't take an Einstein to guess who—or what—had sent it.
>
> From: **The Rats of Wolfe Island**

Read the opening and concluding paragraphs of the two books below. Look for ways the opening and concluding paragraphs tie the story up into a neat unit.

1. *The Strange World of Elmer Floyd*:

Opening paragraph:

> Some things are so strange—so strange that they are really hard to explain.

Closing paragraph:

> 'Yes,' said Elmer. But he thought that there are some things that are really strange—so strange that they are hard to explain.

2. *The Big Race*:

Opening paragraph:

> It shouldn't have been on my mind all night, but I guess it was. I don't know if I was excited—or anxious. Or was it Claws—Claws McGhee?

Closing paragraph:

> I had won. I looked back at Claws. To my amazement he smiled and gave me a tired 'thumbs up' as I tumbled through kids running onto the track to congratulate me.

Exercise 1

(answer page 115)

How have the opening and closing paragraphs been tied together?

____

____

Exercise 2

(answer page 115)

In the extracts from *The Big Race*, there is a change in attitude towards Claws McGhee.

1. How did the narrator (the person telling the story) feel towards Claws in the opening paragraph?

____

2. How did the narrator feel towards Claws in the closing paragraph? ______________

____

Reading task 2

Read the opening and closing paragraphs of *Holly and the Frog Prince* by Elaine Horsfield. The final paragraphs are almost a repeat of the opening paragraphs.

Opening paragraphs:

> Holly's mother read her a story about a princess that kissed a frog. The frog turned into a handsome prince and they got married.
>
> 'Revolting,' said Holly, pulling a face, 'You'd never catch me kissing a yukky frog.'
>
> 'I should hope not,' said her mother kissing her goodnight.

Closing paragraphs:

> That night, she [Holly] hid the Frog Prince book under her bed.
>
> 'Revolting,' she said. 'You won't catch me kissing a yukky frog.'
>
> 'I should hope not,' said her mother as she turned out the light.

Writing task

(answer page 115)

Read this opening paragraph to a story titled 'Cave-in' and then write a concluding paragraph of two or three sentences.

> Narida walked towards the entrance of the old gold mine, then stopped. She peered into the darkness. She could see nothing beyond the first few rotted and broken support beams. She told herself there was nothing to be scared of. Still she hesitated.

____

____

____

____

Endings that upset readers

Here are some types of endings that upset readers:

1. Then I woke up and found it was all just a dream/nightmare.
2. And they lived happily ever after.
3. Suddenly my superhero saved me from [some sort of disaster].
4. I said the magic words and everything was right.

Research

Re-read the last few paragraphs of five books you have read recently and see how, **in your opinion**, the paragraphs round off the story. Label them unsatisfactory, satisfactory or very satisfactory and add a comment. You may have to re-read the first few paragraphs as well.

Book	Opinion of final paragraph(s)
1. ____________	____________________ ____________________
2. ____________	____________________ ____________________

3. ____________	____________
	____________
4. ____________	____________
	____________
5. ____________	____________
____________	____________

Writing tip

Many people, including teachers and competition judges, don't appreciate your adding the words **The End** to the end of your story. It is not necessary.

Using sentence types

Revision

There are four main sentence types, all of which can be used in fiction writing.

Sentence type	Example
1. Statement	Dark clouds filled the morning sky.
2. Question	What is the matter with Fido?
3. Exclamation	Watch out!
4. Command	Put your book on my desk.

Exercise 1

(answer page 115)

Name these sentence types.

1. Jake's father waved an angry fist at the birds circling the field. ______________________

2. Let's get out of here! ______________________

3. Pass your book to the teacher, Graham. ______________________

4. Why do storks build nests on chimney tops? ______________________

5. Put all the mail in the tray on the desk. ______________________

Reading task 1

Read this passage and look for several different sentence types.

Most of the class hurried outside for lunch. Everyone was talking about Mr Long, our new classroom teacher. Was he once an army sergeant? He was worse than that. He was a slave driver!

This morning we had ten minutes to do twenty questions. I just got finished in time. Poor Kerry was still inside slaving over the last four questions.

Sentence type	Sentence example
______________	______________________________
______________	______________________________
______________	______________________________
______________	______________________________

Writing tip

Remember to use a variety of sentence types in your story (not only in speech). Including a sentence that isn't a statement every so often can improve your writing.

Exercise 2

(answer page 115)

Add the correct punctuation to this extract to show which sentences are statements, questions, commands and exclamations. (Some of the sentences can be punctuated in two different ways, depending on how they are used.)

It works, it really works__ I can hardly believe it__ My invention is working__ It has been running for more than three minutes and is still working__ Scientists from all over the world will want to see it__ They will be speechless__ Newspaper reporters will come with their photographers to do feature articles on me__ And what will I tell them__ I will say this is the first fully automatic short story writer__

Writing task 1

Write a paragraph or two using at least two sentence types. A title has been provided. (For this exercise don't use speech in your writing.)

Dad Prepares Breakfast

____

____

____

____

____

Reading task 2

Read this example of writing by Moya Simons. She has made it interesting by using different sentence types.

> Saturday morning. School holidays. Mum is sitting at the breakfast table in her spotted PJs. I am sitting opposite watching a beetle scurrying towards the sugar bowl. Life is full of uncertainty. Do I kill it—thereby wiping out generation after generation of future beetles? I mean, who knows? One might be a special beetle destined to lead insects out of the dark age into the brave new world of tomorrow.
>
> From: **Sit down, Mum, there's something I've got to tell you**

The person who is in the story telling the story is called the **narrator**.
The person who wrote the story is called the **author** (or writer).

Exercise 3

(answer page 115)

Answer these questions based on the above extract.

1. How many sentence types have been used? ______________________

2. The use of questions gives the reader a clue as to how the narrator feels about killing the beetle. What feeling is the narrator experiencing? ______________________

3. The extract actually starts with two incomplete sentences. They are used to 'grab' the reader's attention. How could the two incomplete sentences be combined to make a 'proper' sentence?

____

Using questions

The use of questions puts the reader in the narrator's mind to share his/her feelings and thoughts. For example:

> ***What was coming?*** I wondered. The dull tearing sound continued. I could see the underneath of the train, which was once the roof, splitting open. There was something inside, bursting to get out. ***IT*** was alive!
>
> From: **Monopillar**

Writing task 2

Using the above passage as a guide, write a paragraph or two with the question sentence below as a beginning. Do not reveal what is behind the door. You don't know yet and you want to keep the reader guessing.

What is behind the door?

Using variations in sentence length

Varying the length of the sentences in your story can have a positive effect on the quality of your writing. Different sentence lengths are important for creating special effects in your story, as well as for maintaining reader interest and excitement.

Reading task 1

Read the poorly written passage 1 and compare it with passage 2, which makes use of sentences of different lengths.

1. Pablo hurried to the door of the quiet hut. He kept his back bent and head down. At the door he removed his gloves. Then he gently tapped the wooden door. No sound came from inside the hut. Pablo gently turned the metal door handle. Holding the handle he pushed the door firmly. The door swung open quietly. Pablo quickly stepped back against the wall.
2. With his head down and back bent, Pablo hurried to the door of the quiet hut. After removing his gloves he tapped gently on the wooden door. Silence. Not a sound from inside. Gently he turned the metal door handle and pushed. The door opened. Pablo quickly stepped back against the wall.

Short sentences create tension

Short sentences are usually best for exciting or tense moments in your stories. Longer sentences tend to suit descriptions.

Read this extract as an example of short sentences used to create a sense of pain.

> He was on his knees. They held. His back held, stiff. If I'm asked what happened to me, I'll say ... 'It's a long story!' In agony, painfully slow, grunting, Andres sets his engines going. He whips himself with words, blast you—heave! Gallop, you lazy horse of dung. He was up.
>
> From: **Talking in Whispers** by James Watson

Short sentences create urgency

Short sentences can also create a sense of urgency and desperation.

Read this extract from *The Big Race*. The short sentences are used to create a sense of urgency.

> Claws was pushing himself hard. He nearly stumbled underneath the trees then disappeared from sight. I concentrated on the ground and tried not to panic. I needed to run faster. I increased my speed.
>
> I was gaining on him.

Exercise 1

(answer page 115)

Rewrite these short sentences as one long sentence. You may have to use conjunctions (joining words) and commas.

1. Nellie got out of bed. She found her hairbrush. She went to the mirror.

2. At the sports carnival Neville came third in his race. He came third in the high jump. Neville didn't get a place in the shot put.

3. Molly put a blue pin in the wall map. Then she put in another blue pin. Finally she put a third blue pin near the first two pins.

Exercise 2

(answer page 115)

Rewrite these long sentences as two or three short sentences.

1. The juggler threw the knife into the air when someone in the audience screamed and for a moment his concentration slipped.

2. The house was dark and Ken felt very scared as he listened to the strange noises of the night bush.

3. There are three parts to a triathlon, which begins with running, followed by a swim section in open water and finally a cycling section along public roads.

Writing task

Write an exciting paragraph about the final minutes of a close sporting competition (e.g. football, netball, tennis).

____

____

____

____

Long sentences

Long sentences tend to slow down the pace of the story. They are often used when the characters are sad, worried, waiting patiently or feeling peaceful.

Reading task 2

The following extract relies on longer sentences to create a sense of anxiety and frustration.

Someone has just rung the doorbell and Kat's father has just told her to go to bed. Now read on.

> But Kat stayed where she was even though she could feel her heart thumping so hard she could almost hear it. If this was more of ***her*** problem she would sort it out.
>
> Her father turned on the porch light. His size was such that whoever was outside was hidden from Kat and her mother. They watched him move his head enquiringly from one side to the other, saw him reach forward and shake someone enthusiastically by the hand.

From: **The Sylvia Mystery** by Penny Hall

Writing tip

The smart thing to do is to incorporate the skills learned in Chapter 8 with the skills you have developed from working through this chapter.

Recommendations

Here are just a few books that use sentence lengths effectively. There are many others. There is a space for you to add to the list.

Check out some of these books in your school or class library.

The John Marsden trilogy

Victor Kelleher, *Parkland*

James Watson, *Talking in Whispers*

E.B. White, *Charlotte's Web*

Paul Jennings, *The Cabbage Patch Fib*

Morris Gleitzman, *Two Weeks with the Queen*

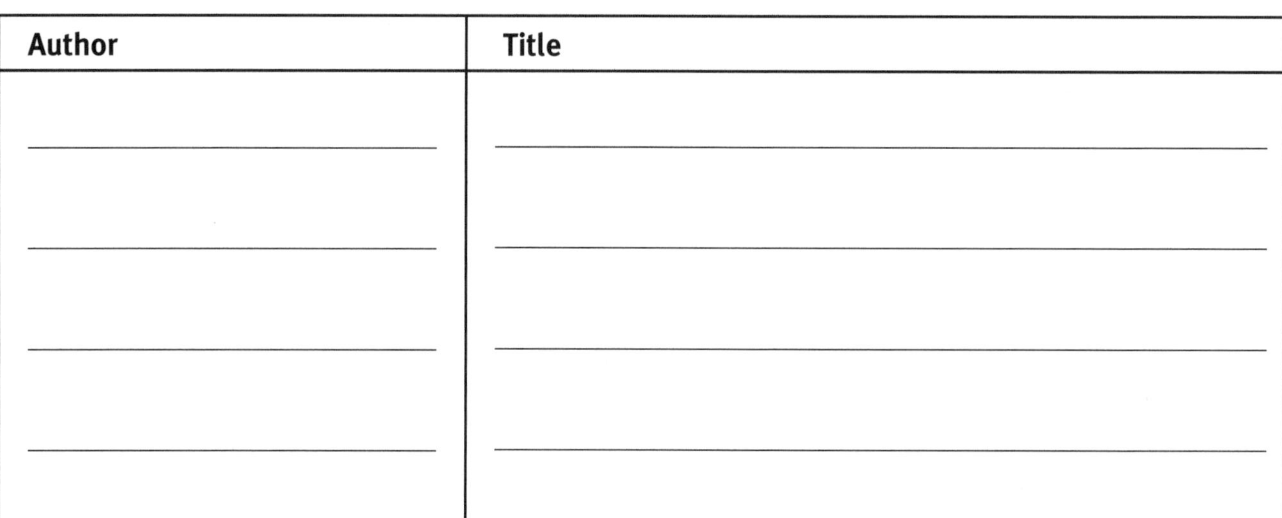

Author	Title

To write in the voice of another language, dialect or social class can be daunting.

In 1991 Diana Kidd wrote the award-winning *The Fat and Juicy Place*. It tells a story from an Aboriginal boy's perspective. It has a very special type of writing. To do this Diana had to get into the 'mind' of the boy and see the world through his eyes. Research for this type of writing is important.

Jack knows a special place behind his school – now read on.

> It's a real good place for testing all them UFOs and Purple Planet missiles I make. Reckon them UFOs go real fast. Faster than the speed of light. True. Like watching them burn through the air into the bushes.
>
> You know what I found there after school today? A lizard. His tail was real long. Never seen a fella as long as that. He only just fitted into my lunch box.

Using variety in sentence beginnings

Here is a quick revision of parts of speech.

Nouns are naming words (e.g. Canberra, cow, crowd, annoyance).

Pronouns are words used instead of a noun (e.g. I, him, her, she, it, them, your).

Prepositions often refer to the position of things (e.g. on, above, beside, past).

Verbs include thinking, doing and saying words, as well as being and having words (e.g. run, running, wonder, shouted, is, had, faint).

Adjectives are describing words that add meaning to a noun (e.g. red, two, cold, sweet, biggest, best, unhappy).

Adverbs tell how, when, where or why something happened (e.g. slowly, soon, here, during, sometimes).

Conjunctions usually join words or phrases (e.g. and, or). Certain conjunctions can be used to start sentences (e.g. although, because, however).

For further information see *Basic Primary Grammar* by P. Walker (Pascal Press).

Writing tip

Use any of the types of words listed above as sentence beginnings. They will add sparkle and interest to your story writing.

Exercise 1

(answer page 115)

The following sentence starts with an adjective.

Dark clouds gathered slowly over the horizon.

Rewrite it, starting with the adverb (**slowly**). (You may make a number of changes.)

____

Now start with the preposition (**over**).

____

Now try the verb (suggestion: change **gathered** to **gathering**.)

____

Reading task

Read this extract from *Aitutaki Phantom* and see how different parts of speech have been used as sentence beginnings.

> Large drops of water began to thud onto the verandah and rattle across the iron roof of the [holiday] cottage. Aaron guessed it was a tropical squall coming in from the ocean, drenching the small outer islands of the lagoon as it came.
>
> Suddenly there was a flash of lightning followed by a clap of thunder just above their cottage. Then the skies opened up and the rain poured down.

Writing task 1

(answer page 115)

Here is a poorly written extract. Rewrite it, using a number of different sentence beginnings. You can change some of the wording but keep the meaning.

> The sun was just coming up over a moon crater. The captain of the spacecraft put on his space suit. The task was slow but finally he was fully suited for a moon-walk. The engineer gave his chief a quick wink as the airlock door opened. The captain entered the airlock and the door hissed closed. The captain was now on his own.

Exercise 1

(answer page 116)

Rewrite these sentences in a more interesting way.

1. Monica had to wait in the dressing shed because she had sprained her wrist.

2. The alien continued and was not deterred by stun guns or laser guns.

____

3. Then it was Fred's turn in the dentist's chair.

____

4. Andrea returned to the camp relying on caution and her common sense.

____

5. The frosty leaves of trees shone in the bright, early morning sunlight.

____

Writing tip

Too many unusual word beginnings can be off-putting to the reader. It's okay to use **the**, **a**, **then**, **he** and so on, just remember to vary your sentence beginnings.

Exercise 2

(answer page 116)

Read the following extract and complete the table below. You will need to recognise the various parts of speech.

> Bob stepped carefully across the scorched ground. Black ash covered the whole lawn. Finally he reached the shed and burnt out remains of his rowing boat. Beside the pile of ash were the mangled remains of a blow torch that had started the fire. His father would be furious.
>
> Suddenly Skye was standing beside him. Nodding her head, she just looked and said nothing. Boats were meant to be in the water she was thinking.

Find sentences that start with the parts of speech listed below. Beside each part of speech write the first word of the sentence. The first one has been done for you.

noun	Bob	preposition	____________
noun	____________	verb	____________
pronoun	____________	adverb	____________
adjective	____________	adverb	____________

Writing tip

The little words **the**, **a** and **an** are often used to start sentences. These words are called articles. Too many sentences starting with these words can make your story monotonous.

Writing task 2

Using the above passage (Bob stepped ...) as a model, write a short passage about discovering a scratch on a new car.

Using repetition

Repetition is another technique of a skilled writer but, like most techniques, you can have too much of a good thing.

Repetition for emphasis

A word can be repeated for emphasis. How does repetition strengthen the meaning? Look at the following sentences and highlight the repeated words.

The sun was very, very red that day.

Boys and more boys tramped into the campsite.

He was tired, so tired that he closed his eyes before they had reached the gate.

Exercise 1

(answer page 116)

Write two of your own sentences, repeating the words **big** and **ants**.

(big) ______________________________

(ants) ______________________________

Repetition to stress a point

A sentence can be repeated to stress a point. Many fairy tales make use of a repeated sentence. Two that come to mind are *The Three Little Pigs* (I'll huff and I'll puff ...) and *Goldilocks* (descriptions of chairs, beds and so on). This gives a sense of rhythm to the story and a feeling of predictability.

In my story for younger readers, *Maria's Coin,* I repeat the sentence 'Once Maria decided to do something she did it' several times throughout the story. This not only provides some rhythm to the story, but it shows the determination of the main character, Maria.

Reading task 1

In another younger children's story I repeat variations of this paragraph using **brown** instead of **white**.

We always have white bread. White bread for toast, white bread for sandwiches, white bread with jam. We always have white bread.

From: **Daily Bread**

How do you think the narrator feels about white bread? ______________________________

Repetition variations

Varying the sentence or phrase can reinforce an idea while advancing your story. Here are two examples.

Coming into the room was an old lady. Leaving the room was an angry nurse.

She had a familiar face, familiar eyes and familiar hair but I could not place where I had seen her.

Select a number of books for younger readers and find examples of repetition in them.

Book/story	Repeated words/phrases/sentences
______________________	____
______________________	____
______________________	____
______________________	____

Flies, flies, flies. They hung around the house all day and all night. It was the smell of the manure. The smell attracted them. There were flies everywhere; they came down the chimney and under the doors. People had no trouble finding our house. If anyone asked where we lived they were always told the same thing. 'Just stop at the house with the flies.'

From: 'Cow Dung Custard', in **Unreal** by Paul Jennings

(answer page 116)

You will have noticed that the word **flies** is not only repeated in the first sentence, it is mentioned several times later in that paragraph.

1. Briefly describe the effect the multiple use of the word **flies** has on you as a reader.

____

____

2. What is the effect of the repetition of the word **all** in the second sentence ('all day and all night')? 'They hung around the house all the time' has almost the same meaning.

Writing task 1

Write your own short paragraph repeating the word **drip** (as from a tap). You might like to model your paragraph on the above paragraph by Paul Jennings.

Writing task 2

(answer page 116)

In each of the following paragraphs select a word that could be repeated to give these sentences more impact. Then rewrite the sentence to show how it has more impact with the repetition.

1. There was sand everywhere. It was in my joggers. Some was in my underpants. There were grains of it in my hair.

Selected word: ____________________

2. Edward could see torch lights through the trees. Several flashed on a nearby rise in the park. Down near the pond beams darted along the edge of the water. Other lights bounced around in the dark foliage of the trees. His pursuers were getting closer.

Selected word: ______________________

___

___

___

Exercise 1

(answer page 116)

Imagine you are in the office of a deserted house without permission. You are searching for something but you don't have much time. You keep checking the clock on the wall.

What word(s) could you repeat to show that the house was quiet and that time was running out?

___

___

Reading task

Read this passage from *Freddie the Frightened* by Pamela Shrapnel.

> Down in the darkened bedroom Penelope was peeping out of the bedclothes with Fred, listening to the tap, tap tapping as the Googyman's cane came closer and closer to the windowsill.
>
> A storm was building up. Perfect Googyman condition, Fred had whispered. Just the weather he needs to finish zapping the window locks.
>
> Tap, tap, tap. Penelope looked across at Fred's trembling head on the other side of the elephant skin boot. Tap, tap, tap, tap, tap, ta*p*, t*ap*, *tap*, *tap*!
>
> A roll of thunder followed a crack of lightning across the house and almost through the room.

What word is repeated to show someone is getting closer? ______________________

Making sense with the senses– 1. Introduction (sight)

Many students rely heavily on what they **see** for their stories. This is important, as sight is one of our most important senses when developing a story.

However, it is not the only sense with which we can take in information.

Exercise 1

(answer page 116)

What are the five senses?

____________ ____________ ____________ ____________ ____________

Look at a piece of your recent writing and see how much you have incorporated a variety of the senses. Use the list above and tick the senses you have used.

Reading task 1

(answer page 116)

Read the following paragraph and work out the sense the author uses.

> At the end of the day Ken was tired, very tired. So tired, in fact, that he couldn't sleep. His legs ached after the climb and his head throbbed from where he had clipped a low branch. The tent was hot and the sleeping bag clammy. Droplets of sweat clung to his forehead. The ground was hard and uneven and he was sure it sloped to one side of the tent.

What sense does the author rely on for his description? ________________________

Reading task 2

(answer page 116)

Read this passage and see how many different senses the author has used.

> Ken struggled down the slope with all the rope he could find on the rusting truck.
>
> He had short bits, long bits, tangled bits and one black length that smelt of oil. Annoying flies buzzed around the weeping gash in his forehead. He paused to look at the track by the dry creek bed and then, licking dust from his dry lips, he pressed on.

What senses has the writer used?

____

(answer page 116)

Look at these brief descriptions of **water** and note the use of different senses:

sparkling water, salty water, stagnant water, chilly water, gurgling water

Describe **pills** and **meat** using several different senses.

__________ pills, __________ pills, __________ pills, __________ pills

__________ meat, __________ meat, __________ meat, __________ meat, __________ meat

Writing tip

Adjectives are effective words for incorporating the senses into your writing. Adjectives are often called describing words. They add meaning to nouns.

Exercise 3

(answer page 116)

Look at the underlined adjectives in this sentence. Write down how they have added meaning to the sentence.

<u>Two</u> <u>scrawny</u> <u>black</u> dogs sat on the <u>dead</u> grass by the <u>back</u> door of the <u>abandoned</u> shed.

____

Exercise 4

(answer page 116)

Add adjectives in the spaces to give this short passage more **sense** appeal.

Ken could see the __________ tent through the __________ scrub. It was on a __________ sandbank near a __________ water hole. __________ smoke curled up from a __________ campfire.

What senses were you able to include in your selection of adjectives?

__________________ __________________ __________________ __________________

Exercise 5

(answer page 116)

In each space write the sense the adjective is portraying. The first has been done for you.

noisy birds	sound	scented envelope	______________
cold steel	______________	sugary biscuit	______________
empty drum	______________	jangling bells	______________
hairy ape	______________	sour cream	______________

Reading and writing task

(answer page 116)

Rewrite the following passage, replacing each underlined **sense** adjective with an adjective referring to another sense. Notice the effect it has on the writing.

> A ~~cold~~ wind whipped through the ~~dead~~ leaves of the ~~slender~~ poplars and across the ~~slippery~~ street. A ~~whistling~~ policeman standing on a ~~deserted~~ corner caught a whiff of ~~decaying~~ garbage.

___

___

___

Writing tip

See Chapter 23 for the use of **see/look** words in your writing.

Reading task 3

(answer page 116)

There are times when a good visual description is sufficient for a story. Read the following passage, answer the question and draw a picture of the room as you visualise it.

> The room was large but there was little in it. In one corner stood a table surrounded by chairs, one leg propped level with the other by a broken wooden crate. On it was an assortment of bowls both plastic and tin, crockery, cooking utensils and a rusty kerosene lamp. Under the only window stood an empty cupboard, while across the room was an untidy assortment of stretcher beds, grey kapok-filled mattresses; pillows and blankets. The only lightness and brightness about the room were the four walls covered with colourful pictures cut from well thumbed magazines, and reed curtains flanking the windows.

From: **Night of the Muttonbirds** by Mary Small

What information about the room do you think the author is conveying to the reader?

Draw your picture of the room here.

Making sense with the senses– 2. What do you feel?

Using the sense of touch can add impact to your story. (In this chapter **feel** refers to physical **touch**, not to the emotions.) When you describe how something feels the reader may be able to bring his/her own understanding to your work.
Look at these sentences:

Steven's fingers touched her cheek. It was cold!

Cold could raise several questions in the reader's mind, including 'Is she dead?' or 'Is it a cold day?'

(answer page 116)

Read this passage and note how the author has made use of the sense of feeling. Highlight the words that refer to feeling/touching.

Fiona made her way across the bare, damp boards of the chilly room. Patches of the floor were so smooth that once or twice she almost slipped. Finally she reached the window. With her finger she rubbed a lop-sided circle in the coating of frost and grime that covered the entire surface. Then, before putting her finger in her warm mouth she rubbed it clean on the coarse fabric of her coat.

Writing tip
Remember, you don't only feel with your hands or fingers. Your whole body is a feeling machine. It feels more than by touch.

Feeling words

Some words that can be used for feeling/touching experiences are:

hot/cold	aches	glare
pressure	wet/dry	
hard/soft	rough/smooth	oily

Feeling isn't always a matter of extremes. Something doesn't have to be hot or cold. There are a lot of words that may go in between these two. Here's another example:

Extreme	Words in between	**Extreme**
agonising,	painful, aching, hurting, sore, tender, soothing,	**pleasant**

You will often find the in-between words are more useful and descriptive.

Exercise 2

(answer page 116)

Fill in your own in-between words for these examples:

wet ______________________________ **dry**

hot ______________________________ **cold**

hard ______________________________ **soft**

Make a list

Keep a list of **feeling** words you might like to use. You can substitute them for words commonly used when you are writing about things you feel.

Here are some to start you off. Add them to your ideas notebook and then continue the list yourself.

rigid	tingling	unevenness	sharp	heavy
numb	brittle	breathless	choking	vertigo

Exercise 3

(answer page 117)

Keep a list of some of the unusual or odd feelings you have had, and what they were. You might be able to use them in your story writing. One has been done for you.

Feeling	What causes it
a sting	a bull ant
____________	____________
____________	____________
____________	____________
____________	____________

Word study 1

(answer page 117)

Use your thesaurus to find two synonyms (words with similar meanings) for each of these feeling words.

rough ____________ ____________

throbbing ____________ ____________

tepid ______________________ ______________________

famished ______________________ ______________________

Word study 2

(answer page 117)

Use your dictionary to find the meaning of these 'feel' words.

harrowing ____

tingle ____

stun ____

drowsy ____

feverish ____

Reading task

(answer page 117)

Read the following passage and find the meanings of the selected **bold** 'feel' words as they are used in the passage.

Borers had attacked the tree, **hardening** the bark into **barbed** knots that made pink **nicks** along Neil's palms as he struggled higher. **Brittle** twigs snapped off, dropping to the ground. Tree climbing was not allowed.

As he grabbed a **roughened** limb his **clammy** fingers slipped, giving him a **start**.

He was about to continue climbing when a wasp dropped from somewhere onto his forearm and **nipped** him angrily. A **searing** pain stabbed his muscle. He couldn't let go to flick it away.

The branch he was standing on started swaying, making him **dizzy**.

The ground below was parched. A fall now would not be onto a **spongy** cushion of grass.

hardening ____

barbed ____

nicks ____

brittle ____

roughened ____

clammy ____

start ____

nipped ____

searing ____

dizzy ____

spongy ____

Note: Any of these words that appeal to you should be added to your ideas notebook.

Making sense with the senses– 3. What do you hear?

Using the sense of hearing can add quite dramatically to your story. In horror stories it can be very effective (though often overdone!).

Reading task 1

(answer page 117)

Read the passage and highlight words that relate to the sense of hearing.

When the laughter of the other campers finally ceased Ken expected silence. He longed for silence. But instead of silence, the bush outside was full of strange sounds.

A bird's mournful cry could be heard in a nearby whispering tree. The monotonous trickle of the creek was like the incessant arguing of a distant group of children. Then he isolated the buzzing and hissing of strange insects, the rustling in the dry grass just by the tent where he was to sleep. He even became aware of his own breathing.

Exercise 1

(answer page 117)

Here is a list of nouns that can be used to describe types of sounds instead of words more commonly used. Add some more words to the list.

echo, din, rattle, scrape, report, bubble, hiss, clang, blare, racket, commotion

________ ________ ________ ________ ________ ________

Including the actual sound

Sometimes it is a good idea to put the actual sound in your story.

Ken sat in his tent, waiting. Every few minutes lightning flashes lit the tent so brightly that he could have read by the light. Still no rain. Maybe it will pass, he hoped. He started to relax.

Boom!

The roar was so close he jumped to his feet.

Exercise 2

(answer page 117)

1. Add to this list of actual sound words you could use in your story writing.

clang, whoosh, tick-tock, oompah, ________ ________ ________

________ ________ ________ ________ ________ ________

2. Keep a list of some of the unusual or odd sounds you have heard, and where you heard them. You might be able to use them in your story writing. One has been done for you.

Sound	Place
the hiss	of car tyres on a wet road
______________	______________
______________	______________
______________	______________
______________	______________

In-between words

Hearing sounds isn't always a matter of extremes. Sounds don't have to be deafening or almost silent. There are a lot of words that go in between the two extremes. For example:

Extreme	Words in between ←——→	Extreme
deafening,	blaring, noisy, loud, distracting, audible, soft, faint,	**silent**

The in-between words are often more accurate and descriptive.

Exercise 3

(answer page 117)

Fill in some in-between words for these examples:

cheep ______________________________ **screech**

thunderclap ______________________________ **snap**

Exercise 4

(answer page 117)

Learn the names of the actual sounds animals make.

What animals make these sounds?

mew ______________ yowl ______________ warble ______________

honk ______________ trumpet ______________ squeak ______________

Word study 1

(answer page 117)

Use your thesaurus to find two synonyms (words with similar meanings) for these **sound** words.

tuneful ____________________ ____________________

rowdy ____________________ ____________________

squawk ____________________ ____________________

rant ____________________ ____________________

Word study 2

(answer page 117)

Use your dictionary to find the meaning for these **sound** words.

whimper ____

bass ____

cooee ____

bay ____

tone deaf ____

Exercise 5

(answer page 117)

What might cause or make these noises?

rattle ____________________ clang ____________________

rumble ____________________ sonic boom ____________________

peal ____________________ chime ____________________

twang ____________________ whine ____________________

Reading task 2

(answer page 117)

Read the following passage and find the meanings of the selected **bold** 'sound' words as they are used in the passage.

> Liz heard the **burble** and the repeated **honking** before she saw the red convertible.
>
> Suddenly the car **screeched** around the corner and came to a stop with a **crunch** of gravel just centimetres from where she stood. The radio **blared**.
>
> It was Brad and she was not amused but all she could do was **splutter** a protest.
>
> Brad pretended to look bored and **snapped** his fingers like a spoilt brat.

burble ______________________________

honking ______________________________

screeched ______________________________

crunch ______________________________

blared ______________________________

splutter ______________________________

snapped ______________________________

Note: Any of these words that appeal to you should be added to your ideas notebook.

Making sense with the senses– 4. What do you smell?

Using the sense of smell can add to the atmosphere of your story. When you describe how something smells it may allow the reader to bring his/her own understanding to your work, as well as evoking a strong mental image in the reader's mind.

(answer page 117)

Compare these sentences and tick the one that has the greater impact.

1. Justin caught a whiff of food cooking. Spicy sausages, or some sort of meat.
2. Justin smelled food cooking. It might be sausages, or some sort of meat.

(answer page 117)

Read this passage and note how the author has made use of the sense of smell. Highlight the words that you feel refer to 'smelling'.

> Randy sniffed twice. The fumes from the bus were upsetting but there was something else. It wasn't a foul smell. It was the trace of a sharp perfume or scent that seemed to sting the inside of his nostrils.

Writing tip

You don't always have to describe the actual smell. You can give the character's reaction to it. Compare these sentences.

Maree held her breath and hurried from the room.

Maree held her nose between her finger and thumb and closed her mouth and eyes.

Maree raised her nose towards the window and smiled.

(answer page 117)

Make a list of nouns that refer to types of smells, pleasant and unpleasant (e.g. stench, aroma).

____

____

Exercise 7

(answer page 115)

Find a single word for these definitions.

1. detect by smelling ______________________

2. removing smells with a deodorant ______________________

Writing task

Poor Chef Coddle is having problems in his kitchen. Using smell-type words from this chapter, describe what might be going wrong.

____

____

____

____

____

____

____

____

Research

(answer page 118)

When someone says 'I smell a rat', what do they mean?

____

____

Note: Any of the 'smell' words that appeal to you should be added to your ideas notebook.

Making sense with the senses– 5. What do you taste?

The sense of taste is one of the least used senses in story writing. It doesn't play a large part in our everyday living. This doesn't mean we are unconcerned about the taste of food we eat. It's more that it's a little less important in most fiction writing. The sense of taste is a very personal sense. Smell and taste are closely related.

There are four basic taste sensations – sweet, sour, bitter and salt – as well as variations of these, such as bland (tasteless) and savoury.

Reading task

(answer page 118)

Read this passage and note how the author has made use of the sense of taste. Highlight the words that you feel refer to tasting.

> Joanna still felt hungry. She continued to sit at the breakfast table looking at her burnt toast spread with butter and sickly, sweet honey. What would she give for something a little bit savoury? Maybe a mouth-watering bite of a spicy hamburger with the tang of Spanish onions.

Writing tip

You don't always have to describe the actual taste. You can give the character's reaction to it.

Compare these sentences.

April put some food into her mouth and chewed it slowly.

April took a morsel of sauce, held it in her mouth for five seconds and then winced.

Exercise 1

(answer page 118)

Can you add to this list of verbs for taste-type actions?

nibble, savour, ____________ ____________ ____________ ____________ ____________

____________ ____________ ____________ ____________ ____________ ____________

Exercise 2

(answer page 118)

Adjectives (describing words) that describe tastes are useful in your writing. Choose words that these adjectives might describe.

delicious ____________ tasteless ____________ hot (spicy) ____________

stale ____________ minty ____________ sour ____________

Exercise 3

(answer page 118)

Add to this list of taste-type adjectives

appetising, tasty, sickly sweet, ____________ ____________ ____________

Exercise 4

(answer page 118)

Give one or two suitable taste-type words that you could use when writing about these foods or drink. The first has been done for you.

Object	Taste words
chilli peppers	spicy, hot
watery cordial	____________
baked chicken	____________

Word study 1

(answer page 118)

Use your thesaurus to find one or two synonyms (words with similar meanings) for these taste-type words.

unripe ____________ ____________

bitter ____________ ____________

appetising ____________________ ____________________

sample ____________________ ____________________

Word study 2

(answer page 118)

Use your dictionary to find the meaning of these taste-type words.

aftertaste ____

taste buds ____

flat ____

sweet tooth ____

Writing task 1

Write a paragraph about the taste of a meal you enjoyed or didn't enjoy.

____

____

____

____

____

____

Exercise 5

(answer page 118)

What animals would you associate with these eating actions?

pecking ____________ lapping ____________ gnawing ____________

Writing task 2

You have just got a job on Old Macdonald's Farm. One of your tasks is to feed the animals each afternoon. Use the above words and other animal eating action words to describe your experiences.

Feeding Time on the Farm

____

____

____

____

____

____

____

____

Research

(answer page 114)

When someone complains that a certain incident has 'left a bad taste in their mouth', what do they mean?

____

____

____

Exercise 6

(answer page 118)

List five tasting words (nouns, verbs or adjectives) you could use for these foods.

______________ ______________

______________ ______________ ______________

Creating characters

The characters in your stories may be good or bad people, criminals or angels. Many writers base their characters loosely on people they know. Characters have physical appearance, habits, emotions and a cultural heritage that makes each one unique.

Writing tip

Some writers make a list of the physical features of each of their characters (e.g. freckles, bald, stubby). Another way of keeping track of the characters' features is to cut a picture of the type of character you want from a magazine, newspaper or comic and keep it near your story writing.

Exercise 1 **(answer page 117)**

Give one character feature of Harry Potter (author: J.K. Rowling). ______________________

Give one character feature of Bugs Bunny (TV cartoon character). ______________________

Using real people

Basing a fictional character on a known person has hidden dangers, especially as you get older and your writing becomes more public. If people recognise themselves in your story and you have been unfairly critical of them, then you just might get sued.

Most of the characters in my longer books are based loosely on real people. I decide on a certain type of person (grumpy, giggly, thoughtful, irresponsible, off-hand) and then I select a particular 'body' for that character. Next, I start changing things to make the character fictional and more interesting but I keep a mental picture of the person. Finally, I decide on a name (see Chapter 18).

Be consistent

The most important thing is for your description of your character to be consistent. Sudden changes in character upset the reader. If your character starts off as cowardly, then don't give them sudden, unexpected moments of bravery. There have to be 'real' reasons for character changes.

(answer page 118)

Complete the table on page 64 by creating some characters. Don't name the real person you have selected. **Said words** refers to how the person would say something. **Went words** refers to how the person might walk or move. (See Chapters 22, 23 and 24.)

Type	Real person	Gender	Age	Shape	Said words	Went words
quiet	Alan H	M	50+	chubby	suggest	stroll
bragging	X					
bully	X					
clumsy	X					
fragile	X					

Of course, you can add a lot more points. One of my characters always wore a red scarf. Another one joked a lot. Another was a little bit accident-prone.

Exercise 3

(answer page 118)

1. Select a character type to suit these **went words**. One has been done for you.

hobble old man

sneak ______________________

stagger ______________________

stumble ______________________

dawdle ______________________

hurry ______________________

2. Select a character type to suit these **said words**.

ordered ______________________

demanded ______________________

pleaded ______________________

whined ______________________

mumbled ______________________

stuttered ______________________

3. Select a character type to suit these **look words**.

peep ______________________

spy ______________________

stare ______________________

study ______________________

gape ______________________

glance ______________________

Checklist for developing characters

Many writers use a checklist (often called a **characterisation tool**) to make sure they are clear about each character. This is one checklist:

- → Physical appearance
- → Movements, gestures and habits (good and bad)
- → Behaviour towards others
- → Attitude to others/attitude of other characters to the character
- → Dialogue (way he/she speaks)
- → Physical environment/setting/where he/she lives
- → Character's past
- → Minor features (name, preferred clothing, favourite TV shows/foods)

(answer page 118)

Use this table to fill in some details of two characters you might write about.

Checklist point	Male character	Female character
Physical appearance		
Movements		
Behaviour to others		
Dialogue		
Physical environment		
Character's past		
Name		

Using the environment

The environment a character is placed in can also give an indication of his or her tastes. A person who keeps plastic flowers in a vase would be a different sort of person from one who always buys real flowers.

The age of a character may also be indicated by the physical surroundings.

(answer page 118)

In this exercise, try to work out the general age (very young, primary school, teenage, young adult, middle aged, elderly) and gender of each person from their surroundings. The first is done for you.

Setting	Age	Gender
A small bedroom with a writing desk, a wall full of pictures of ponies	Primary school	Female
A fast food outlet about 4 pm, character buying a large hamburger	____________	__________
A seat near the front row of the ballet, the character wearing diamonds	____________	__________
A lifesaver sitting in a lookout chair during summer	____________	__________

Exercise 6

)

Write some points about each of these characters. Give the character a name.

Name: ____

Likes: ____

____

Dislikes: ____

Occupation: ____

Name: ____

Likes: ____

____

Dislikes: ____

____

Occupation: ____

Giving characters names

Some writers sweat over the names of the characters in their stories. Getting the right sounding name can be important. Christine or Christopher might not be suitable for a child from a place such as India or China.

I try to find names that suit the character. I have an old farmer called Clarry. I would never call a child Clarry. It's just too old fashioned. Elmer Floyd from *The Strange World of Elmer Floyd* was a bit of an odd-ball.

Exercise 1 **(answer page 118)**

Highlight the names you think are more suitable for adults in your stories. Remember, names can go in and out of fashion.

Edward	Elsie	Jake	Wilma	Jenny	Theodore
May	Kathy	Guy	Dee	Skye	Doreen

Exercise 2 **(answer page 119)**

With children you can often get away with nicknames: Blue, Ginger, Skip, Macca. List some fun nicknames you know.

_______________ _______________ _______________ _______________ _______________

Names and more names

I often look for unusual names. Here are some names I have used in my stories: Aaron, Jedd, Nellie, Hannah, Buster, Claws (Claude), Jason, Connie, Loren, Harley.

You can also be adventurous. You can skip the Johns and Marys if you wish. There are lots of unusual names about now, names such as Storm, Tiger Lily, Reef, Cyclone, Rainbow, Magic.

I have three books of names. The good thing about name books is that they give the meaning or origin of names. I have a character call Brian. Brian means brave, but my Brian is only brave in his daydreams! I have a character called Calvin, which means bald. He was the hair robber in *The Great Hair Robbery*. I have another older character called Rex – Rex King (in *The Rats of Wolfe Island*). He is a lone scientist on an island. Rex is another word for king.

Writing tip

It may be wise to check out what your character's name actually means.

Exercise 3

(answer page 119)

Make a list of two or three names you might use later for:

Older males: ______________________________

Older females: ______________________________

Younger people: ______________________________

Mischievous children: ______________________________

Unusual characters: ______________________________

Writing tip

A good place for finding names is in the credits of a movie (that part at the end where they list everybody that ever had anything to do with the movie).

For interesting last names I often look up the telephone directory. That's how I found the family name (surname) Twentyman that I used in *The Ghost Writer.*

Research

Using a telephone directory find five unusual family names that you could use.

__________ __________ __________ __________ __________

Writing tip

It's important to avoid using character names that sound or look similar – Godfrey and Geoffrey; Lorna and Laura. Similar sounding names may confuse your reader.

Fun names

For some characters **alliteration** (words that start with the same sound) and **rhyming** are useful tools in giving a hint to how you want your reader to interpret the character. It would be hard to take Molly Jolley (rhyming) seriously. Julie Judge (alliteration) might be a little more serious.

Of course, you can have real fun with names like Sandy Shaw, Crystal Ball, Rocky Hills, Penny Farthing, Rose Bush, Bob Downes, Roxanne Stone, Isabel Silver.

Exercise 4

(answer page 119)

1. Invent three or four characters whose first and last names rhyme.

2. Invent three or four characters whose first and last names are examples of alliteration.

Exercise 5

Invent names for each of these people and then give a brief description of their character.

Name:

Character:

Name:

Character:

Name:

Character:

Name:

Character:

Giving characters real character

Some student writers have no fixed idea in their minds of just what goes into being a person. It is sometimes said that their characters are 2D (two dimensional, or flat) and not 3D (three dimensional, or developed). They have no depth. They are there for the plot and don't have any other reason for existing.

Before you start writing, imagine what makes your character tick. Is he/she shy, confident, thoughtful, caring, moody and so on? And, of course, the character may not be like that throughout the whole story. A caring character may be stirred to anger by a thoughtless act!

List some types of characters you could include in your story. Two are given to start you off.

brave, miserly __________, __________, __________, __________, __________, __________,

__________, __________, __________, __________, __________, __________

Being consistent

Once you have decided on your character's character you have to make sure his/her actions and speech reflect that type of character. How would a lonely man react in a busy shop? How would a timid girl react in a new school?

Although your characters should behave **consistently** they do not have to display their main characteristic all the time. A grumpy person is allowed to smile. A quiet person might be stirred to make a noise by excitement or anger.

(answer page 119)

Look at the table on page 71. Next to the character types, write down a behaviour you might expect from them. The first two have been done for you.

Character type	Action
bold	speaks loudly
lazy	leaves clothes on the floor
thoughtful	________________
cheerful	________________
selfish	________________
clumsy	________________
disorganised	________________
restless	________________

Exercise 3

(answer page 119)

Remember, you don't have to tell the reader what sort of character the person has. You can let the reader work that out from the behaviour of the character.

1. How would you describe the character in this short passage?

   Andrew knew what to do. He put his dirty dishes on the sink. He wiped the table where he had been sitting and pushed the chair in, without scratching the floor. After switching off the kitchen light he went to the bathroom to clean his teeth.

   ____

2. There can be shades of character types. List some character types that could go between a

   calm person and an **angry** person. ________________

Using speech

One of the most important ways a person's character is shown is by what they say and how they say it (see Chapter 22).

Look at this sentence: 'I'm going home,' said Margie. It tells the reader very little.

Let's change it to: 'I'm going home,' snapped Margie. This has much more impact.

How about: 'Going home!' growled Margie.

I'm sure you can see differences.

Now compare these characters showing their annoyance:

'Stop doing that,' said Janet.

'Do you mind?' hissed Penny.

The second example provides readers with more information than the first example.

Exercise 4

(answer page 119)

1. Write your own 'said' words in the spaces and note how the meaning changes.

'I can't do that,' ______________ Alvin. 'I can't do that,' ______________ Alvin.

'I can't do that,' ______________ Alvin. 'I can't do that,' ______________ Alvin.

2. Put suitable 'said' words in the spaces for the speakers. Try to imagine the situation in which they might say the words.

'What are you doing here?' ______________________ the school teacher.

'What are you doing here?' ______________________ her best friend.

'What are you doing here?' ______________________ my mother as she came into my room.

'What are you doing here?' ______________________ the swimming coach.

Reading task 1

How might different people tell someone to leave a room? Look at these examples:

'Get out of here at once!' snarled my big sister.
'Get lost!' ordered Oliver.
'You may be excused,' smiled the teacher.
'No children allowed in here,' advised the museum attendant.
'Take those smelly pups out of here right now,' cautioned the grim-faced nurse.
'You are no longer welcome,' warned the librarian.

Showing differences

Different characters also speak in different ways. Some people speak quickly, some mumble, some have 'bad' speech. Here are a few ways people might speak:

softly, carefully, with a lisp, with a stutter, with unfinished sentences, repeating themselves, rudely

See if you can add to the list. ______________ ______________ ______________

Reading task 2

Read this extract and note how the people speak in different ways.

> The next day Mum placed her just-baked bread onto the table. We all shook our heads as she cut it. It was ... green!
>
> 'Guess what?' she said.
>
> 'Beans?' I guessed.
>
> 'Peas?' said Connie.
>
> 'Lettuce?' whispered Loren.
>
> 'No, no, no,' laughed Mum. 'It's cabbage bread!'
>
> From: **Daily Bread**

Revision

When there is a **change of speaker** in your writing you should start a **new paragraph**.

Writing task

Write two pieces of conversation using three different 'said' words.

1. Said words: ________________ ________________ ________________

____

____

____

____

____

2. Said words: ________________ ________________ ________________

____

____

____

____

____

Showing, not telling

Many writers try to tell the reader too much and often too quickly. As stated earlier, readers are intelligent people with imagination and experiences. A good writer will allow their readers to use these.

Exercise 1

(answer page 119)

Compare these two passages.

1. Leslie crept up to the door and listened for several seconds. Then she heard it. A strange scraping sound. She knew what was in the pantry.
2. Leslie crept up to the door of the pantry and listened for a few seconds before she heard the scraping sound of hungry mice.

Which example best draws the reader into the story? ______________________________

Why? ______________________________

Reading task 1

Look at this sentence:

The sky was patched with grey clouds and they were getting darker by the minute.

What is happening? Most likely, there is a storm coming.

The writer could have written: A severe storm was quickly approaching.

Exercise 2

(answer page 119)

Read these sentences and briefly answer the questions with your own reactions.

1. Dad was pulling on the handbrake. His knuckles were white.

What is about to happen? ______________________________

What is Dad feeling? ______________________________

2. The small yacht *Flying Fish* bounced about in the choppy seas. The captain was lying on his bunk in his cabin. A small, empty bottle was rolling around the floor.

Why is the captain lying on his bunk? ______________________________

What has been in the bottle? ______________________________

What is the weather like? ______________________________

3. Anthony came to the water's edge. He looked into the blackness and shivered.

Why does Anthony shiver? ______________________________

Exercise 3

(answer page 119)

Add a sentence to each of the examples below to **show** the feeling in brackets. For example:

Mary was just finishing the question when she saw Brett looking over her shoulder. (annoyance)
She tapped the end of her biro noisily on the desk.

1. Ken heard the wind whistle through the pines. (cold) ______________________________

____

2. Greg handed a folded piece of paper to the teacher. (worry) ______________________________

____

3. Ms Moggs entered the classroom for the first time. (nervousness) ______________________________

____

4. Father came in from work at 8 o'clock. (fatigue) ______________________________

____

5. I searched but could not find the silver button. (embarrassment) ______________________________

____

6. The coach watched his team enter the court. (pride) ______________________________

____

7. Peter opened the exam booklet and read the first question. (relief) ______________________

____

8. After placing the vase on the table Jenny stepped back. (satisfaction) ______________________

____

Exercise 4

(answer page 119)

Now try the same exercise, but this time show different responses to the same lead-in sentence.

Turning the corner, Brett saw three dogs a short way off. (fear) ______________________

____

Turning the corner, Brett saw three dogs a short way off. (surprise) ______________________

____

Turning the corner, Brett saw three dogs a short way off. (pleasure) ______________________

____

Turning the corner, Brett saw three dogs a short way off. (confusion) ______________________

____

____

____

Reading and writing task

(answer page 119)

The following sentences are examples of **showing, not telling**. Read each example and then answer the question.

1. Moths made lazy circles around the streetlights.

What time of the day is it? ______________________

2. The men pulled in their nets as the boat rocked gently.

What are the men doing? ____________________

3. When Sylvia turned the corner into the main street she stopped. It was deserted.

What might Sylvia be feeling? ____________________

4. A group of youths turned to face the sound of the siren, then looked at each other.

Why do the youths look at each other? ____________________

5. Sandy suddenly jumped to his feet. Squealing, he brushed his legs frantically.

What is on Sandy's legs? ____________________

6. The teacher came into the empty room, shook his head and then scratched it.

What is the teacher feeling? ____________________

Reading task 2

(answer page 119)

Read the extract and briefly answer the questions. The answers are **not** in the extract.

> The room was large but there was little in it. In one corner stood a table surrounded by chairs, one leg propped level with the other by a broken wooden crate. On it was an assortment of bowls both plastic and tin, crockery, cooking utensils and a rusty kerosene lamp. Under the only window stood an empty cupboard, while across the room was an untidy assortment of stretcher beds, grey kapok-filled mattresses, pillows and blankets.
>
> From: **Night of the Muttonbirds** by Mary Small

1. Has the building been occupied recently? ____________________

2. Where is the building situated? ____________________

3. What kind of people use the building? ____________________

Selecting a point of view

Before you start writing you should consider who is telling the story.

First person

If your story is in first person, that is, the narrator is telling the story, then the story is from his/her viewpoint. In first person narrative the writer uses the words (pronouns) **I**, **me** and **we** often throughout the story.

Read this short passage written in **first person**. (The personal pronouns are in **bold**.)

> The marathon had just started and **our** team was near the front. **I** heard the gun blast to start the race and **we** were off! **I** dropped in behind Greg who was **our** team leader even though **I** was the best marathon runner in **our** team. And if it hadn't been for **me**, **we** would not have been in the race at all!

First person stories

If your story is in first person, then all the action is limited to what the narrator can see, hear and experience. It is impossible to see into the minds of other characters but first person narrative can create closer contact with the reader. Diary-type stories are in first person. They are personal records of events and feelings (e.g. *So Much to Tell You* by John Marsden, *Penny Pollard's Diary* by Robyn Klein).

(answer page 114)

Go to your library and find two books written in **first person**.

Examples are *Treasure Island* by Robert Louis Stevenson and *The Gizmo* by Paul Jennings.

Find a copy of *Lake at the End of the World* by Caroline Macdonald. The story is told in first person from two different viewpoints. How has Caroline organised this?

___

___

___

Third person

Many stories are told in third person from the viewpoint of one or more of the characters. They are told as if the reader is watching what events are happening and what is going on in the character's mind. *Charlotte's Web*, by E.B. White, is told from Charlotte's viewpoint and at times from Fern's viewpoint, in alternating chapters.

In your stories, you may take the 'overall' viewpoint. The main character often sees or knows what is going on in other people's minds. Changes in setting are easily brought into the story.

Writing tip

The danger with the 'overall' approach is that the writer can give *too* much away, not allowing the readers to draw on their experiences and imagination.

Reading and writing task

There is about to be an accident on the intersection of Main St and High St. There are at least ten people somehow involved in the event. In a few sentences write what is happening from three different points of view. Select a character from each category. Before you start writing read the sample passage to help you understand what is required.

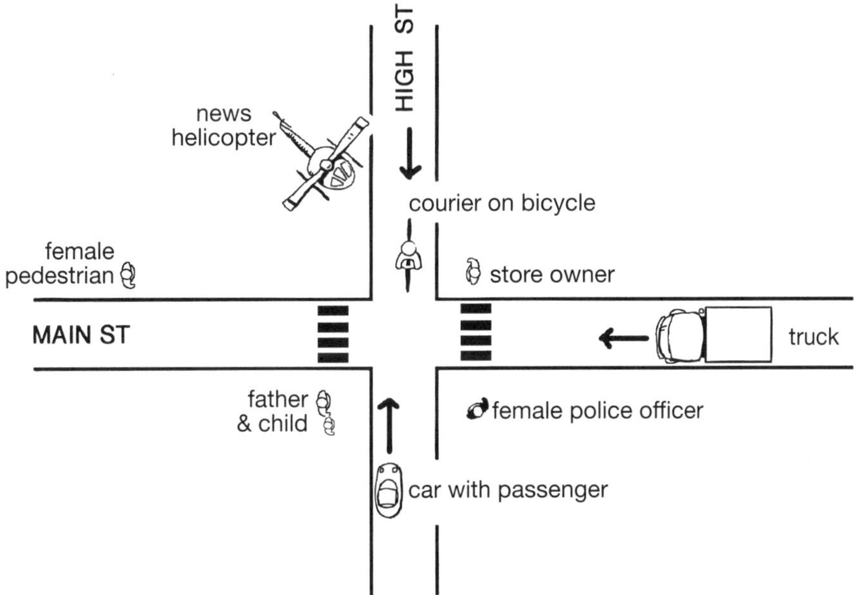

1. Third person: driver of truck, driver of car, father, child, passenger

Sample of writing in the third person:

'Captain, we've got to get him to a doctor. Or a hospital.'

Aaron could sense the urgency in the man's voice.

Charlie started wheezing again. The bout lasted several minutes. The boat rocked.

'Steady on, fellow. There must be help here somewhere,' the man in the boat muttered, trying to calm Charlie.

From: **Aitutaki Phantom**

2. First person: female police officer, female pedestrian, store owner, child, courier

Sample of writing in the first person:

> Climbing into the cabin I saw just how much damage was done. This is no accident, this is vandalism, I thought.
>
> The driver's seat was slashed. The radio unit was sprayed with black paint.
>
> I needed to find another van in a hurry.

3. 'Overall viewpoint': the news reporter in the helicopter

Sample of writing using an overall viewpoint:

> Cindy crossed the ridge and began walking down the northern slope. She had no idea where Leanne could be. It worried her.
>
> Leanne was still by the creek. She hadn't been able to move since she had twisted her ankle. She bathed it in a cool pool.
>
> Meanwhile, out of sight of both girls, storm clouds were building up behind the range. Neither girl was aware of the dangerous situation that could quickly develop.

Finding other words for said

In any speech in your story writing it is very easy and convenient to use the word **said**. It can also become monotonous (see Chapter 19).

I try to find said-type words that contain shades of meaning in the way a speaker is talking. For example, consider these words: whispered, murmured, hissed, sighed, breathed. They are all examples of speaking softly but each one carries its own additional information.

Writing tip

A good **thesaurus** is a must! Many computer programs have a built-in thesaurus but I find these fairly basic (as yet). You also still need a dictionary.

Reading task

Read these sentences and consider the way the speaker has said them.

'That was the last game I will ever play in this team,' **growled** the suspended player.
'That was the last game I will ever play in this team,' **sighed** the retiring player.
'That was the last game I will ever play in this team,' **admitted** the injured goalie.
'That was the last game I will ever play in this team,' **teased** the captain.

Notice how much more impact the bold words have than **said** would. They give the reader some idea of the speaker's feelings and attitude. They also give the reader some insight into the character of the speaker.

Exercise 1

(answer page 119)

Find a variety of suitable said-type words to complete these sentences.

1. 'Turn that motor off now!' ________________ the foreman.

2. 'Oh, I hope that's not more bad news,' ________________ the upset mother.

3. 'I will pay you a million dollars for that shirt,' ________________ my father.

4. 'But you aren't listening to my complaint,' ________________ the customer.

5. 'Give it back!' ________________ the new student.

Sentence order

The quoted words of the speaker need not start the sentence. For variety, the quoted words can come after we are told who is speaking. Compare these two sentences.

'It is now time to select the winners,' announced the judge.
The judge announced, 'It is now time to select the winners.'

(answer page 119)

Rewrite these sentences with the quoted words starting the sentence.

1. Bill suggested, 'Your truck should be moved off the footpath.'

____

2. Dad joked, 'You now owe me one hundred dollars.'

____

Exercise 3

I have a list of words that I like as alternatives to 'said'. Here is an alphabetical selection. There are spaces for you to add your own 'said' words.

a. answered ____________________

b. bawled ____________________

c. cried ____________________

d. denied ____________________

e. explained ____________________

f. forgave ____________________

g. greeted ____________________

h. hinted ____________________

i. implied ____________________

j. joked ____________________

k. kidded ____________________

l. laughed ____________________

m. muttered ____________________

n. niggled ____________________

o. offered ____________________

p. prayed ____________________

q. quipped ____________________

r. roared ____________________

s. sneered ____________________

t. teased ____________________

u. uttered ____________________

v. volunteered ____________________

w. whined ____________________

x. ? ____________________

y. yapped ____________________

z. zapped ____________________

Word study

(answer page 120)

Use your dictionary to find the meaning of these 'said' words.

preach ____

rant ____

state ____

claim ____

confirm ____

chide ____

Writing task

(answer page 120)

Fill the spaces in this short passage with a variety of different said-type words. Make your 'said' word suit the character or the situation.

'Do you think we are lost?' __________________ Peter, looking at the broken sign.

'I hope not,' __________________ Penny, shaking her head.

'Let me see the compass. Maybe you got it wrong,' __________________ Peter angrily.

'But I only did it the way you told me,' __________________ Penny, glaring at him.

Reading and writing task

Read the following passage. It relies heavily on the use of **said**.

'What day is it?' said Vicki.
'Wednesday,' said her mother.
'Surely not,' said Vicki.
Her mother said, 'It's been Wednesday all day.'
'Oh,' said Vicki, 'I was supposed to hand in a project.'
'Don't tell me you forgot?' said her mother.

In the two copies below 'said' has been deleted.

Fill in the blanks in **Copy 1** with 'said' words that show a friendly relationship between Vicki and her mother.

Fill in the blanks in **Copy 2** with 'said' words that show a stressful relationship between Vicki and her mother.

Copy 1

'What day is it,?' ______________ Vicki.

'Wednesday,' ______________ her mother.

'Surely not,' ______________ Vicki.

Her mother ______________, 'It's been Wednesday all day.'

'Oh,' ______________ Vicki, 'I was supposed to hand in a project.'

'Don't tell me you forgot?' ______________ her mother.

Copy 2

'What day is it,?' ______________ Vicki.

'Wednesday,' ______________ her mother.

'Surely not,' ______________ Vicki.

Her mother ______________, 'It's been Wednesday all day.'

'Oh,' ______________ Vicki, 'I was supposed to hand in a project.'

'Don't tell me you forgot?' ______________ her mother.

Finding other words for 'look'

Just as the overuse of 'said' can become monotonous and uninformative, to a lesser extent the same can be said for **look** words, as well as a number of other words (see also Chapters 19, 22 and 24).

Reading task 1

Read these look-type sentences and consider how the character acted.

My father **studied** a report in a business magazine.
The teacher **glanced** into the classroom as he passed on his way to the office.
Lynne **inspected** the apple in her lunchbox .
The goalie **glared** at the coach for allowing the penalty.
The tired hikers **surveyed** the valley below, looking for signs of habitation.

Notice how much more impact the bold words have than 'looked' would have. They give the reader some idea of the speaker's feelings and attitude. They also give the reader some insight into the character of the 'looker'.

Exercise 1

(answer page 120)

Find a variety of suitable look-type words to complete these sentences.

1. Mr Rufus ____________________ at the class over his half frame glasses.

2. The detective ____________________ a small brooch in the dying grass.

3. Jake ____________________ at the small print on the menu in the dim cafe.

4. Dr Jackson ____________________ the behaviour of the rats in their cages.

5. Kerry had a quick ____________________ at the book on her mother's desk.

3. The driver ____________ the track, which was being covered with floodwater.

4. The driver ____________ the track, which was being covered with floodwater.

5. The driver ____________ the track, which was being covered with floodwater.

Reading task 3

(answer page 120)

Highlight all the look-type words in this passage.

Peter and his sister, Gail, stood outside the toyshop window. They gazed in wonder at the colourful display. Surveying the toys available, Peter wondered what he might get for Christmas. Then he spied a multi-coloured space ship. He could picture the machine sitting on his homework desk.

Gail eyed a book with pop-up pictures. It was open at the middle page and she could make out goblins sitting under giant toadstools. They had large saucer-like eyes that seemed to stare out at her.

Neither child suspected that they were being quietly observed by their father.

Exercise 5

(answer page 120)

Find a suitable look-type word to describe what these people might be doing. The first has been done for you.

Example: a detective secretly watching a suspect (spying)

1. a doctor looking at an X-ray ____________________

2. a shooter looking at a target ____________________

3. a boy looking for a lost marble ____________________

4. a bystander watching a crime ____________________

5. an old person trying to read small print ____________________

Research

(answer page 120)

Find the meaning of these terms.

1. look daggers ________________________________

2. rubbernecking ________________________________

3. drop one's eyes ________________________________

Finding other words for 'went'

Just as 'said' and 'look' can be overused, so can **went** (see also Chapters 19, 22 and 23).

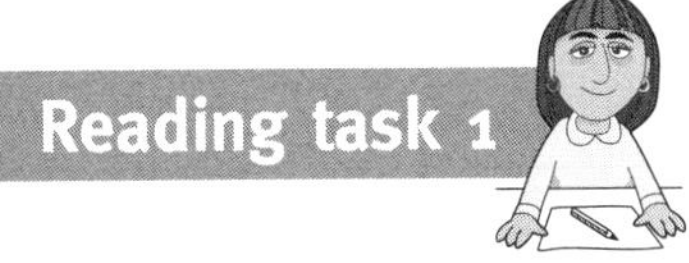

Reading task 1

Read these went-type sentences and consider how the character acted.

My great-grandfather **shuffled** down the hallway to the bathroom.
The guard **marched** the prisoner back to his cell.
Lenny **wandered** down to the post office to check the mail.
The lone explorer **staggered** into the campsite battered and weary.
Farmer Jones **plodded** across the wet fields.

Notice how much more impact the bold words have than **went** or similar words would have had. They give the reader some insight into the character's feelings and attitude.

Exercise 1

(answer page 120)

Find a variety of suitable **went** words to complete these sentences.

1. Our dog, Scruffy, ________________ across the park to greet my sister.

2. The scouts ________________ across the shallow lake to the campsite.

3. The small birds ________________ from one flower to the next.

4. Simone rented a canoe and ________________ across the bay.

5. The class, hot and weary, ________________ all the way to the oval.

Exercise 2

(answer page 121)

What word(s) might describe how this player is travelling?

____

____

Word study

(answer page 121)

Use your dictionary to find the meanings of these **went** words and terms.

trundle ______________________________

ramble ______________________________

twirl ______________________________

file ______________________________

thread ______________________________

rolling stone ______________________________

Writing tip

Look for words that show different ways a character might get from one place to another on foot (e.g. walked, ambled, strolled, hiked). They are all examples of 'walking' but each one carries its own additional information.

In the same way there are different words for travelling across water and through the air.

Exercise 3

(answer page 120)

Make your own alphabetical list of words that are alternatives to **went**.

a. ambled ____________	**h.** hiked ____________
b. ____________	**i.** ____________
c. ____________	**j.** ____________
d. ____________	**k.** ____________
e. ____________	**l.** limped ____________
f. ____________	**m.** ____________
g. ____________	**n.** ____________

o. ______

p. ______

q. ______

r. ______

s. strolled ______

t. ______

u. ______

v. ______

w. walked ______

x. ______

y. ______

z. zoomed ______

Reading task 2

How is the meaning of these sentences changed by the different went-type words?

Peter **crept** through the tall grass on his way to the deserted house.
Peter **barged** through the tall grass on his way to the deserted house.
Peter **struggled** through the tall grass on his way to the deserted house.

Exercise 4

(answer page 121)

Using the words in your list above, fill in the blanks in these sentences to give different meanings.

1. The pirate ______ along the wharf until he found his boat.
2. The pirate ______ along the wharf until he found his boat.
3. The pirate ______ along the wharf until he found his boat.
4. The pirate ______ along the wharf until he found his boat.
5. The pirate ______ along the wharf until he found his boat.

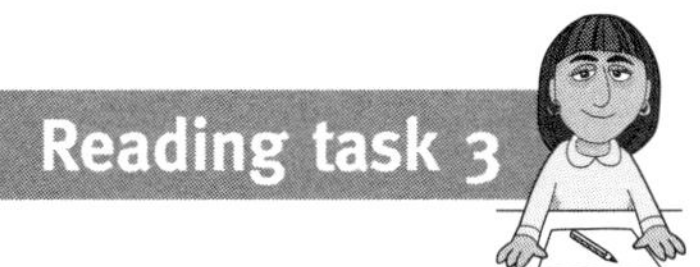

Reading task 3

(answer page 121)

Highlight all the **went/walked** words in this passage.

Mr Joseph hurried from the store. He was late for his appointment and he'd have to run to the bus stop. He skipped around a lady wheeling a pram and dodged past a courier slipping out of a doorway. Then he stumbled.

Ignoring the looks of bystanders, he crawled quickly to his feet and limped to the bus stop, only to see the bus chugging into the streaming traffic.

He turned around and hobbled off to find a taxi.

Exercise 5

(answer page 120)

Find a suitable **went/walked** word to describe these movements.

Example: a bushwalker (hike)

1. a robber going down an alley ______________________

2. a cat hunting for mice ______________________

3. a person on in-line blades ______________________

4. a parent aware of a sleeping child ______________________

5. a bee going quickly from flower to flower ______________________

Research

(answer page 114)

Find the meaning of these terms.

1. run amok ____

2. helter-skelter ____

3. drag one's feet ____

Structuring a story

Most stories start with some sort of problem, such as bullying, a murder, finding treasure, getting a boy/girl friend.

This problem has to be solved. Along the way to solving the problem a number of events take place. These are sometimes called obstacles, complications or crises. I often have three of these in a story. Finally, the problem is resolved at the climax.

Writing tip

The climax should be the most exciting part of your story. That is where the problem is solved in some way (not necessarily happily).

Story structure

Here is a simple diagram for story writing. All stories do not have to follow this structure.

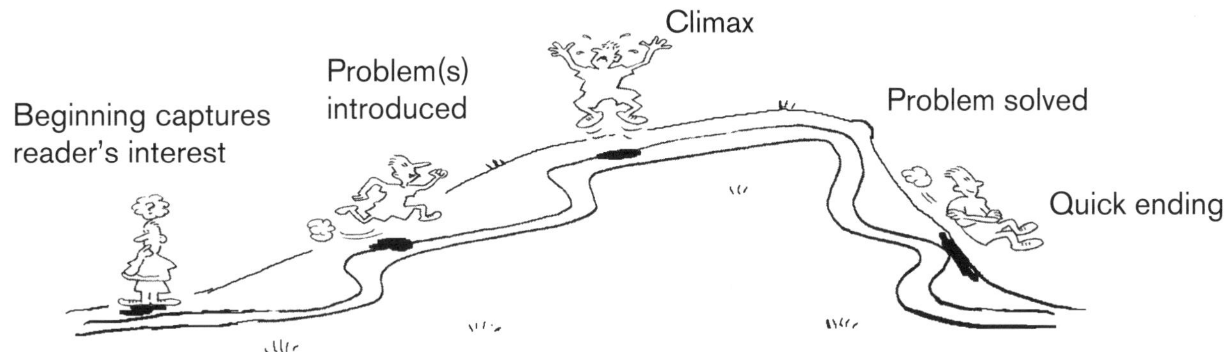

This is the structure of the story *My Sad Skeleton*.

Beginning: Jed opens a box, which contains a skeleton (his father is an archaeologist).

Problem: The skeleton is sad and lonely. Jed decides to help the skeleton.

Complications:

1. Jed and the skeleton go for a walk in the park, hoping for inspiration to make the skeleton happy. They are chased out by hungry dogs.
2. Jed and the skeleton go to a museum to look for ways to make the skeleton happy. They are chased by museum guards who think Jed is robbing them of an exhibit.

Climax: Jed and the skeleton go to a fun fair in an effort to make the skeleton happy. They are confronted by an 'angry' sideshow operator.

Resolution: The skeleton gets a job scaring people riding on the ghost train.

Quick conclusion: Jed and his father wave to the skeleton when the fair is in town.

Writing tip

The complications on the way to the climax should become increasingly difficult to solve.

Exercise 1 (answer page 121)

Take the fairy tale *Little Red Riding Hood* and jot down the points of its structure, as in the example of *My Sad Skeleton*.

Beginning: ____________________

Problem: ____________________

Complications: ____________________

____

Climax: ____________________

Resolution: ____________________

Writing an outline

An outline is a short description of the plot of the story that you intend to write. For school assignments you may keep the outline in your head. For longer works and for special situations (exams, projects, competitions) it is wise to write the outline on a piece of paper. You can change it along the way if you come up with different ideas.

The outline for *Goldilocks and the Three Bears* might go like this:

> Girl goes for early morning walk in the woods. Discovers an empty house and makes herself at home. Eats food, breaks furniture and goes to sleep in a bed. Owners (three bears) return and are upset by what they see. Discover girl asleep. Girl wakes up, jumps out the window and escapes.

Exercise 2 (answer page 121)

Write a brief outline for the fable *The Hare and the Tortoise*.

____

____

Reading task

(answer page 121)

Can you name the fables based on these outlines?

1. A mouse disturbs a lion, which threatens to eat it. The mouse begs forgiveness and offers to repay the lion for kindness. The lion laughs at the offer but releases the mouse. The lion gets trapped in a net. The mouse frees the lion by gnawing through the net. The lion and the mouse become friends.

2. A mouse living in the country invites a town cousin to visit him. Though his lifestyle is simple he is generous and courteous. When the town mouse experiences country life he is appalled. He explains how dull country life is compared to his town life and invites his cousin to town. The home in town is luxurious and the country mouse begins to wonder if he could ever again be content in the country. Before long town dangers change his mind.

3. A grasshopper is amazed by the way ants work all summer collecting food when so much food is always available. He scorns the ants for their industry. He spends his time enjoying himself. When winter arrives, the grasshopper becomes hungry and cold but the ants have plenty of food. They have no sympathy for the grasshopper.

(answer page 121)

Write a brief outline for the fairytale *Jack and the Beanstalk*.

Move the story forward

A story must move forward. It should move forward with more than just incident after incident. We have all seen movies where the main character goes from one 'disaster' to another. These often do little to progress the story. Just how many wild aliens can an astronaut fight before the end of the film? We get that 'oh-not-again' feeling.

In a good story each crisis/complication moves the story forward. For example, in *The Three Little Pigs*, each new 'house' situation is more complicated than the previous one. Finally the desperate wolf has a plan that may succeed.

Using metaphors, similes and clichés

In class you may have been told about metaphors, similes and clichés. Here's a quick reminder.

A **simile** is when we say something is similar to something else, often using 'like' or 'as'. Example: The snake was like a partly coiled rope lying in the sun.

A **metaphor** is when we identify something in terms of another object. Example: The snake was a partly coiled rope lying in the sun.

A **cliché** is an expression that has been overused or overworked. Examples: The cake was as flat as a tack. I smell a rat!

Writing tip

Metaphors and similes are two of the main tools of figurative language. They should be used with care. Too many can be off-putting for the reader and can sound false.

Exercise 1 (answer page 121)

Highlight the **similes** in this short passage.

Although the blossoms were as red as blood now, by nightfall they would be like used bandages. Craig wondered if he should have bought plastic flowers. At least they didn't curl up and wilt like fairy floss in the hot sun. Trouble was they looked as phoney as the set of a school play.

Exercise 2 (answer page 121)

Highlight the **metaphors** in this passage.

Joan's bedroom was a pigsty. In the far corner was a pile of dirty clothes waiting to do battle with any individual who might even consider removing them to the laundry. The hastily discarded school exercise books made a variety of badly built pyramids on her desk.

Single word metaphors

Sometimes a single word can act as a metaphor. Consider the effect of the bold words.

The car **sailed** down the highway.

Jim **bulldozed** his way down the field before being pulled down.

It was a **tired** little stream that **wandered** across the flat fields.

Countless satellite dishes **looked** towards the heavens.

Exercise 2

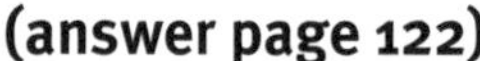

(answer page 122)

Highlight the word(s) in brackets that create a metaphor for each of these sentences.

1. Every big city is no more than (an overgrown town, a jungle, a maze of streets).
2. One of the twins was a lion, the other was (a lamb, a boy, fat).
3. The (straight, golden, long) path to happiness is difficult to find.

Warning!

Don't mix metaphors. They can sound ludicrous. For example:

In the modern world rat race it's dog eat dog.

To succeed you must keep your nose to the grindstone and your head held high.

Reading task

(answer page 122)

Similes can give impact to your writing. If you were writing a ghost story, tick the simile that would be most appropriate.

☐ He entered the room that was as dark as the inside of the kitchen cupboard.

☐ He entered the room that was as dark as a crypt on a winter's night.

☐ He entered the room that was as dark as the finest chocolate he had ever eaten.

Writing task

(answer page 122)

Use similes to finish these sentences and create different impressions in the reader's mind.

Gwen took the letter from the letterbox as if it were ______________________________.

Gwen took the letter from the letterbox as if it were ______________________________.

Gwen took the letter from the letterbox as if it were ______________________________.

Warning!

Similes do not always have to be at the end of the sentence. For example: Like a snake, Roderick was ready to strike the enemy.

Exercise 4

(answer page 122)

Suggest alternative similes for the similes in **bold** in this short passage. Write your suggestions in the spaces.

Dead branches, like **bony fingers and arms** (________________________________) reached for the sky. Growth abnormalities on the trunks looked like **the distorted faces of deformed puppets** (________________________________). Ancient bushfire burns reminded Shane of **dried black scabs on a pale skin** (________________________________).

Exercise 5

(answer page 122)

Write similes to describe these pieces of machinery.

1. helicopter ____
2. locomotive ____
3. space station ____

Extension

Here is a **sustained metaphor**. It is an image that is carried on for more than one sentence. In this example the metaphor is carried on for several lines of the poem.

White sheep, white sheep,
On a blue hill,
When the wind stops
You all stand still.
When the wind blows
You all run away,
White sheep, white sheep,
Why don't you stay?

Extension exercise 1

(answer page 122)

1. What are the 'white sheep'? ________________________
2. Where can they be seen? ________________________

3. Draw a small picture to illustrate the poem.

Extension exercise 2

Using 'White Sheep' as a model, write your own poem using a **sustained metaphor**.

Some suggested topics are:

- → describe a red bushfire as a dragon
- → describe a cement truck as an elephant
- → describe an excavator as a dinosaur

(Title) ______________________

Using different text types

Text types are simply different ways of presenting the written word. A newspaper report is quite different from a film review.

In many stories, using different text types can add variety to your story telling, highlight a particular point and allow you to avoid long descriptions. For example, when I found it difficult to describe a school burning down I made up a **newspaper report** to record the event. I have never seen a school burn down. The report in the paper let me comment on the frightening event without the detail.

I have found I can give a quick run down on a character by looking at their **business card**.

Look at the business card below and note how quickly it gives a lot of information.

Exercise 1

(answer page 122)

From information on the card what are two things you might say about Alan Smith?

1. ______________________________

2. ______________________________

Exercise 2

This is a list of some of the text types I have used in stories. Tick any you have recently used.

Newspaper reports
Business cards
Fliers
Posters
Play reviews
Emails
Faxes
Historical records
Maps
Sets of rules
Instructions
Sketches
Advertisements
Letters
Programs
Classified ads
Memos
Drama scripts
Recorded messages
Postcards
Shop front signs
Graffiti
Words of a song
Poetry

Here are a few more I haven't used – yet.

Comic strips
Cartoons
Diaries
Timetables
Editorials
Photographs
Recipes

Example

Different text types also allow the reader to bring different information to your story.

In the story *My Sad Skeleton*, I used a flier (notice) similar to this one. It was found in the family letterbox.

The flier allowed me to give a lot of information and impressions of the fair without going into lengthy detail.

(answer page 118)

What are three facts or impressions you get about the fun fair from the flier?

1. ______________________________

____

2. ______________________________

____

3. ______________________________

(answer page 114)

Using different text types is not new. In *Treasure Island,* Robert Louis Stevenson uses the words of a song, a letter and a map.

1. In *Harry Potter and the Philosopher's Stone* by J.K. Rowling, Chapter 6, Harry finds a card inside the wrapper for a chocolate frog. What sort of card is it? (Tick one.)

   Sports card Witch/wizard card Free frog card Magic trick instructions

2. Look in some books you have recently read and find examples of where different text types are used.

Exercise 6

Create a flier (letterbox notice) for a fictitious event to be held in your locality.

The event is being arranged to get the Blackthorn School into the *Guinness Book of Records* as well as to raise money. The organisers want as many volunteers as possible to join hands to make a huge human circle.

Writing task

Write a few sentences about the experiences of one of the organisers trying to get some boys and girls to hold hands.

Looking at the features of a story

Here is a short story. Read it and then look for examples of writing techniques used.

Oops, Wrong Choice!

Chapter 1

Last holidays I found a notice in our mailbox.

> Make the Scene Green
> Help the neighbourhood
> and the environment.
> Plant some greenery now.

I showed my parents.

'Great idea!' declared Dad.

'We could do something in our yard,' said Mum.

Harley said, 'But I'm on holidays.'

'We can all care for ***one*** plant!' declared Mum.

'Easy,' agreed Dad. He found paper and a pen. He wrote down our names and next to each name he wrote the person's choice.

Mum	waterlily
Harley	cactus
Dad	palm tree
Jasmine	African violets

As you can see Mum likes pretty plants, Harley likes to be way-out and Dad always does things in a big way.

They thought my idea of African violets for my windowsill was odd, but Dad agreed and with a knowing smile said, 'Oops, wrong choice, I think?'

Before anyone could change their mind Dad phoned Anything Grows Nursery with our order.

Chapter 2

Later a truck from Anything Grows backed up our drive. Dad's palm tree stuck up over the cab. It had long fronds and six brown coconuts.

It was hoisted off the truck and placed in a hole near our swimming pool. Dad was all smiles.

Mum's waterlily was put in a new plastic pond near her rockery. Mum was all smiles.

Then the driver hauled a big, spiky cactus in a huge earthenware tub from the truck. Harley was pleased.

The driver looked at me with a puzzled frown. I didn't have my plant!

Suddenly he remembered. My plant was in the cab.

I was handed a small pot plant with blue flowers with a very delicate scent.

And I smiled!

Chapter 3

Next day, Dad made a cold drink and sat down in his deckchair in the shade of his palm. After finishing his drink he stood up to have a stretch by the pool.

Luckily he did. A large coconut fell from the palm, landed on his canvas chair, bounced into the air like a football and collected Dad just behind the knees.

Dad crumpled into the pool with a mighty splash. He came up spluttering. When he saw the coconut floating nearby he growled, 'That tree has got to go!'

Next day Anything Grows came with their digger to take the tree away.

Oops, wrong choice! I thought.

Mum's lily was okay until she added goldfish to the pond.

One morning when Mum had finished feeding her fish our cat decided it was time for some self-help. It snuck up to the rockery, then made its dash.

Trouble was the cat thought the big flat lily pads were unsinkable. Without hesitating it jumped from the rocks onto one. The lily pad buckled and suddenly the cat was scrambling around in the pond trying to get up the slippery sides.

'Mum!' I yelled.

Mum came rushing to rescue her cat. The cat was upset. So was Mum.

When she saw the mess in her pond she sighed, 'That pond has to go!'

Later, Anything Grows came to take the pond away.

I just said softly, 'Oops, wrong choice!'

Chapter 4

When Harley was playing with his ball it went behind his cactus. He pulled the pot from the wall.

Trouble was Dad had just come into the yard when something in the grass caught his eye. As he bent over he backed straight into Harley's cactus. He got such a fright he yelled, grabbed his backside and stumbled into the pool.

When he stopped splashing about he glared at Harley. Harley shuffled up to the pool to say, 'Sorry.'

Dad shouted, 'When did you move that plant?'

Harley backed away from his fuming father – right into his own cactus! He got such a fright he yelled, grabbed his backside and stumbled into the pool with Dad.

As they clambered out they agreed the cactus had to go.

Anything Grows took it away.

I just smiled to myself, 'Oops, wrong choice!'

Then Mum, Dad and Harley came into my room. They looked at my African violet.

I waited. Would my plant have to go back to Anything Grows?

Dad nodded, 'Neat plant. Won't knock anyone over.'

Harley said, 'It hasn't got spikes!"

Mum said, 'It is pretty.'

Now we all have African violets. Good choice!

Respond to the following. Answers are on page 122.

1. Find an example of repetition of a phrase or sentence. ______________________

____

2. What text type, other than narrative, is used in the story? ______________________

3. Find an example of the use of the sense of smell. ______________________________

4. Find an example of the use of the sense of feel. ______________________________

5. Find an example of a simile. ______________________________

6. Make a comment about the title. ______________________________

7. Make a comment about the last line. ______________________________

8. List some words used instead of 'said'. ______________________________

9. How would you describe the father? ______________________________

____

10. What words/actions helped you draw this conclusion? ______________________________

____

11. How would you describe Jasmine? ______________________________

____

12. What words/actions helped you draw this conclusion? ______________________________

____

13. In your opinion is Jasmine a suitable name for the daughter? ______________________________

____

14. Give two examples of concrete detail. ______________________________

____

15. Find an example of a short sentence. ______________________________

16. Who made the most sensible plant choice? ______________________________

Story writing checklist

Use this checklist to see how many of the features described in this book you have used in your stories. Tick any features you have used.

It is not necessary to incorporate all the features explained in this book to have a successful story. In fact, to include them all in one story might not lead to good story writing.

Feature	**Your story title**							
	1	2	3	4	5	6	7	8
Good title								
Use of concrete detail								
Interesting opening paragraph(s)								
Satisfying closing paragraph(s)								
Variety of sentence types								
Variety of sentence lengths								
Variety of sentence beginnings								
Use of repetition								
Using more than one of the senses								
Well-chosen character types								
Well-chosen character names								
Character/s well developed								
Showing, not telling								
Point of view considered								
Words other than 'said', 'went' and 'looked'								
Developed plot with climax								
Use of metaphors and/or similes								
Use of different text types								
Use of new/interesting words								

Collecting words for a 'good word' list

Many writers make a point of keeping a record of interesting and exciting words that they find. These are not necessarily new words but words they have more or less forgotten or don't use in everyday conversation.

Here are three I found recently that I have used:

slew: It means to twist and turn as cars might do on ice.

raddled: It means unkempt (untidy) and run down in appearance.

feisty: It carries a sense of assertiveness and aggressiveness with it. Someone described a young girl in one of my stories as feisty. I had forgotten the word but it was spot on.

In this space keep a list of words that may come in useful later on. It may be wise to give brief definitions or show how they are used.

Reference books for student writers

Every writer must have a dictionary. Don't rely only on your PC's word-check.

These are some of the books I have. Many were picked up in suburban markets, second-hand bookstores and remaindered book stores. Some of these may be in your family book collection.

You don't need to buy these books but the list gives you some idea of how writers operate.

- Several dictionaries (my big one is too heavy to carry around!)
- Several thesauruses (one in dictionary order of words and a comprehensive one such as Roget's)
- The Australian *Style Manual*
- *Fowler's Modern English Usage*
- *Common Errors in English*
- Several books of quotes (it's wise to know who wrote any quote you use)
- A book of euphemisms
- A dictionary of proverbs
- A dictionary of omens and superstitions
- An illustrated book of traditional symbols
- Several books on words (anagrams, palindromes)
- Three books of names (and their meanings)
- Several basic atlases and maps
- A book on birds of the world (for precise descriptions)
- Several books on children's literature
- Numerous travel guides and maps

My suggestions of a **basic collection** for a serious writer starting out are:

- A good dictionary
- A thesaurus
- A guide to correct grammar/punctuation
- A basic grammar book (e.g. *Basic Primary Grammar* by P. Walker, Pascal Press)
- An atlas
- A book of common errors in English
- A book of names

Writing tip

If your interest in writing is with 'truck' stories then you should have some basic reference books about trucks. Know the correct word.

What is a road train? ______________________________

Top twelve tips for aspiring authors

1. To become a competent writer you need to practise. The more you practise the better you will become (just like a golfer or swimmer).
2. Enter your work in competitions. Competitions have guidelines that will make you look more critically at your efforts.
3. Don't be afraid of not getting it right first attempt. All authors have rewritten pages of their work because the first try didn't sound right.
4. Keep a notebook for ideas always handy. Write your ideas down no matter how silly they might sound at the time. Who would have thought a story about a talking spider (*Charlotte's Web*) would make a million dollars? The Paddington Bear books started with a very simple idea.
5. Read a variety of books/authors on the subject matter that interests you as a writer. Maybe someone has already written a similar story. Maybe you can write a better version of the story.
6. Don't forget that personal experiences are an important source of information.
7. When you are writing and the story seems to want to jump from your brain to the page don't worry about spelling, grammar, capital letters and so on. If you are 'on a roll' they can be corrected later.
8. Don't worry about starting with a title. It will pop into your head later.
9. Make sure you have a dictionary and a thesaurus handy.
10. Don't be afraid of criticism (or rejection slips from publishers).
11. Listen to authors talking about their writing experiences. Many schools have visiting authors and writing workshops.
12. Let the imagination run free.

33 Further reading

Basic Primary Grammar, P. Walker, Pascal Press, 1996 edition

Handbook for New Writers, John Hays, John Hays Publications, 1985

Glossary of selected terms

adjective describing word (e.g. 'big')

adverb word that adds meaning to verbs (e.g. drove slowly, returned soon)

alliteration words starting with the same sound (e.g. 'splutter, splash')

article the words 'a', 'an' and 'the'

atmosphere the mood aroused by a story (e.g. foreboding, peacefulness)

audience people who read text

author creator of a story (or text)

character 1. a person in a story 2. the qualities of a person

cliché overused word/phrase (e.g. 'dead as a doornail')

climax most exciting part of a story, always close to the end

command sentence that directs an action (e.g. 'Give it to me.')

complication (in plot) a problem that must be solved or overcome

concrete detail actual objects, places (e.g. 'a Pepsi', rather than 'a drink')

conjunction joining word (e.g. 'and', 'but', 'or')

contrast (in titles) terms that do not usually go together (e.g. 'Hot Ice')

dialogue the words characters say

exclamation sentence that is abrupt or excited comment (e.g. 'That hurts!')

first person text written from the viewpoint of the narrator; uses the pronoun 'I' (e.g. 'I came home late.')

gender male or female

metaphor describe one thing as another (e.g. 'the army tank was a dinosaur')

narrative (text) text that tells a story

narrator the person in a story telling the story – not the author

noun name of person, place or thing

outline brief summary of a story

paragraph sentences in a story that focus on one feature/detail in the story

plot the story plan of a book (or film)

preposition word that gives position (e.g. 'by', 'near')

pronoun word that replaces a noun (e.g. 'he' for 'Jim')

publication allowing others to read created text, including posters, books, charts

pun a play on words/double meaning (e.g. Why did the toad cross the road? To see his flat mate.)

question sentence that seeks an answer

recount retelling events as they occur

repetition repeating of words and sounds for effect (e.g. 'Ants and more ants!')
resolution the solving of a problem
rhyme words with similar sounds (e.g. 'cat' and 'hat')
second person text that is directed to the reader; makes use of 'you' (e.g. 'You put on a hat.')
simile describing something as being like something else (e.g. 'as cold as ice')
statement sentence where something is revealed (e.g. 'Jan is six years old.')
sustained metaphor a metaphor that is carried on for several sentences
teasers titles that create 'false' impressions
text meaningful (written) communication
text types varieties of text (e.g. plays, poems)
third person text written about other people (e.g. 'Betty has a balloon.')
verb a word that tells an action or a state (e.g. 'was', 'run', 'driving')

For more detail see *Basic Primary Grammar* by P. Walker (Pascal Press).

Answers

Note: The answers given for many of the exercises and tasks are suggestions only. You may have thought of other acceptable responses.

1 Writing narratives Page 1

Exercise 1

recount, narrative

Exercise 2

trudged, no avail, brisk, explored, silent, strolled

Reading task

incomplete sentences, description, atmosphere (branches that look like naked arms)

2 Recognising where ideas for stories come from Page 4

Student responses

3 Writing what you know – first-hand experiences Page 7

Exercise 5

Internet, library, reference books, DVDs, magazines

Exercise 6

Tortoise – shelled reptile with clawed limbs; turtle – aquatic, shelled reptile with flippers

Research

1. incorrect; 2. correct; 3. correct; 4. incorrect; 5. correct

4 Choosing titles (What's in a name) Page 11

Exercise 1

murder mystery, detective story, thriller, adults

Writing task 1

younger children

Exercise 4

(suggestions) Sudden Storm; Adopt an Alien; Desert Dust; Who Stole My Stripes?; Flowers on the Grave; Backchat

5 Knowing the importance of detail – concrete or general? Page 15

Exercise 1

vehicle – utility; tree – poplar; jam – strawberry jam; drink – flavoured milk; house – red brick house; magazine – ***TV Times***; TV show – Bugs Bunny; flower – daisy; film – ***Star Wars***; fish – flathead; ball – tennis; neighbour – Mrs Smith

Writing task 1

1. The ginger cat sat on the Persian carpet. 2. Paul took ***Nature World*** from the magazine rack to the check-out counter.

Exercise 2

dinghy, boxes and bundles, shouldered, dragging

Writing task 2

1. The school's top football team cheered the visiting Welsh players who had just beaten the home team.
2. The black flies were crawling all over the sausages and salad that had been set out for their end-of-term picnic.
3. Julie bit into her bacon and egg pie after smothering it in chilli sauce pie. She then washed it down with a large gulp of Pepsi.
4. The flock of young merinos roamed over the barren hills in search of dry grass.
5. The gusty wind and chilling rain lashed the yachting clubhouse for nearly two hours.
6. The roar of a rebel tank in the town sent residents hurrying for the meagre protection of their temporary homes.
7. A man in a tracksuit hesitated by the ancient headstone and read the damaged inscription.

8. As the Riverside Rockers started playing 'Down by the Riverside' the teenage audience drowned out their words.

6 Creating opening paragraphs that capture the reader's interest Page 19

Exercise 1

What ad? Why is the narrator waiting? Where is the narrator waiting?

Exercise 2

What are Cindy and Craig looking at? Where are they going?

Exercise 3

It was one of the most embarrassing moments of my whole life when I won the set of pink baby's clothes in the school raffle. And I don't even like girls, big or little. And what did my friend Kevin do? Laugh, then rush off to tell all the boys in the soccer team.

There are usually fifteen boys who turn up for training. Today twenty-five turned up, including Mad Mike McMahon.

7 Choosing closing paragraphs Page 23

Exercise 1

They both have similar wording.

Exercise 2

1. afraid/anxious; 2. unafraid/amazed

Writing task

Narida turned the last corner of the old gold mine. She saw the oval of sunlight that meant freedom. As she left the opening she didn't bother to look back.

8 Using sentence types Page 27

Exercise 1

1. statement; 2. exclamation; 3. command; 4. question; 5. command

Exercise 2

(Some variations possible)

It works, it really works! I can hardly believe it. My invention is working. It has been running for more than three minutes and is still working. Scientists from all over the world will want to see it. They will be speechless. Newspaper reporters will come with their photographers to do feature articles on me. And what will I tell them? I will say this is the first fully automatic short story writer.

Exercise 3

1. two; 2. indecision/reluctance; 3. It was Saturday morning and school holidays.

9 Using variations in sentence length Page 31

Exercise 1

1. Nellie got out of bed, found her hairbrush and went to the mirror.
2. At the sports carnival Neville came third in his race and high jump but didn't get a place in the shot put.
3. Molly put three blue pins in the wall map near each other.

Exercise 2

1. The juggler threw the knife into the air. Someone in the audience screamed. For a moment his concentration slipped.
2. The house was dark. Ken felt very scared. There were strange noises in the night bush.
3. There are three parts to a triathlon. It begins with running, followed by a swim section in open water. A cycling section along public roads completes the event.

10 Using variety in sentence beginnings Page 35

Exercise 1

Slowly dark clouds gathered over the horizon. Over the horizon dark clouds slowly gathered. Gathering over the horizon were dark clouds.

Writing task 1

Coming up over a moon crater was the early morning sun. The captain of the spacecraft put on his space suit. Slowly but finally the task was completed and he was fully suited for a moon-walk. There was a quick wink from the engineer for his chief as the airlock door opened. After the captain entered the airlock door hissed closed. The captain was now on his own.

Exercise 2

1. Because she had sprained her wrist

Monica had to wait in the dressing shed.

2. Not deterred by stun guns or laser guns the alien continued to advance.
3. Fred had the next turn in the dentist's chair.
4. Relying on caution and her common sense Andrea returned to the camp.
5. Shining in the bright, early morning sunlight were the frosty leaves of trees.

Exercise 3

noun – Bob; noun – boat; pronoun – his; adjective – black; preposition – beside; verb – nodding; adverb – suddenly; adverb – finally

11 Using repetition Page 39

Exercise 1

Big men and big women filled the gym. Ants, ants and more ants swarmed across the picnic cloth.

Exercise 2

1. Repetition of the word 'flies' makes the reader think of many flies.
2. Repetition of the word 'all' enforces the idea that it was a long time.

Writing task 2

1. (sand) There was sand everywhere. Sand was in my joggers. Sand was in my underpants. There were grains of sand in my hair.
2. (lights) Edward could see torch lights through the trees. Several lights flashed on a nearby rise in the park. Down near the pond lights darted along the edge of the water. Other lights bounced around in the dark foliage of the trees. His pursuers were getting closer.

Exercise 3

tick-tock

12 Making sense with the senses – 1. Introduction (sight) Page 43

Exercise 1

sight, sound, smell, touch, taste

Reading task 1

feeling (touch)

Reading task 2

hearing, smelling, feeling, tasting, seeing

Exercise 2

rattling pills, bitter pills, pink pills, smooth pills, peppery meat, red meat, greasy meat, rotten meat, sizzling meat

Exercise 3

They give a clearer picture of the situation.

Exercise 4

Ken could see the tattered tent through the parched scrub. It was on a damp sandbank near a stagnant water hole. Blue smoke curled up from a warm campfire.

Exercise 5

noisy birds (sound); cold steel (touch); empty drum (sight); hairy ape (sight/touch); scented envelope (smell); sugary biscuit (taste); jangling bells (sound); sour cream (taste)

Reading and writing task

A fresh wind whipped through the rattling leaves of the yellowing poplars and across the dusty street. A stout policeman standing on a noisy corner caught a whiff of scattered garbage.

Reading task 3

the desolation of the place

13 Making sense with the senses – 2. What do you feel? Page 47

Exercise 1

Fiona made her way across the bare, damp boards of the chilly room. Patches of the floor were so smooth that once or twice she almost slipped. Finally she reached the window. With her finger she rubbed a lop-sided circle in the coating of frost and grime that covered the entire surface. Then, before putting her finger in her warm mouth she rubbed it clean on the coarse fabric of her coat.

Exercise 2

wet, soggy, damp, moist, dry; hot, warm, cool, chilly, cold; hard, firm, pliable, soft

Exercise 3

sting of a bull ant; prick of a pin; itch of hives; tingle of cold fingers; vibrations of power tools

Word study 1

rough – uneven, jagged; throbbing – thumping, pounding, tepid – lukewarm, warmish; famished – hungry, ravenous

Word study 2

harrowing – agonising or distressing; tingle – a prickly, itchy sensation of the flesh; stun – to make unconscious by a heavy blow; drowsy – getting sleepy; feverish – a body condition of high temperature and fast pulse

Reading task

hardening – becoming harder; barbed – sharply pointed; nicks – small cuts; brittle – easily snapped; roughened – made rough; clammy – unpleasantly sticky or damp; start – a fright; nipped – pinched; searing – burning; dizzy – giddy, unsteady; spongy – soft and rubbery (elastic)

14 Making sense with the senses – 3. What do you hear? Page 51

Reading task 1

When the laughter of the other campers finally ceased Ken expected silence. He longed for silence. But instead of silence, the bush outside was full of strange sounds. A bird's mournful cry could be heard in a nearby whispering tree. The monotonous trickle of the creek was like the incessant arguing of a distant group of children. Then he isolated the buzzing and hissing of strange insects, the rustling in the dry grass just by the tent where he was to sleep. He even became aware of his own breathing.

Exercise 1

rattle, hush, gurgle, screech, melody

Exercise 2

1. boing, beep, pop, toot, put-put; 2. hiss of car tyres on a wet road; drone of an aircraft; splutter of a motor; tinkle of piano keys; chimes of a clock

Exercise 3

cheep, chirp, squeak, scream screech; thunderclap, blast, crack, pop, snap

Exercise 4

mew – cat/seagull; yowl – cat; warble – magpie; honk – goose; trumpet – elephant; squeak – mouse

Word study 1

tuneful – musical, melodic; rowdy – noisy, disorderly; squawk – shriek, howl; rant – rage, rave

Word study 2

whimper – sob softly; bass – lowest male singing voice; cooee – call used to attract attention; bay – a deep long howl; tone deaf – lacking ability to detect differences in musical notes

Exercise 5

rattle – chains; clang – warning bells; rumble – thunder; sonic boom – jet; peal – bells; chime – clock; twang – guitar string; whine – engine

Reading task 2

burble – soft bubbling sound; honking – sound like a goose; screeched – made loud piercing sound; crunch – crisp brittle sound; blared – make a loud harsh noise; splutter – make an explosive noise; snapped – make a sharp short sound

15 Making sense with the senses – 4. What do you smell? Page 55

Exercise 1

(a)

Reading task

Randy sniffed twice. The fumes from the bus were upsetting but there was something else. It wasn't a foul smell. It was the trace of a sharp perfume or scent that seemed to sting the inside of his nostrils.

Exercise 2

pong, fragrance, stink, scent

Exercise 3

smoky, strong, odourless, fruity, musky, spicy

Exercise 4

fumigate, reek, detect

Exercise 5

old clothes – musty, damp; swamp – foul, putrid; pine needles – fragrant, scented

Exercise 6

fragrant rose, rancid meat, spicy sauce, stale air, smoky clothes, fruity cordial

Word study 1

putrid – rotten, rank; waft – drift, float; smelly – stinking, pungent; foul – repellent, putrid; aromatic – fragrant, perfumed

Word study 2

nauseating – causing a person to feel sick; whiff – a mild passing odour/a single inhalation of a smell; fumes – smells given off by some (chemical) reaction; deodorise – to remove or disguise (unpleasant) smells; high – smelling stronger than usual; off – smelling rotten

Exercise 7

1. sniff; 2. deodorise

Research

I suspect someone of doing evil.

16 Making sense with the senses – 5. What do you taste? Page 59

Reading task

Joanna still felt hungry. She continued to sit at the breakfast table looking at her burnt toast spread with butter and sickly, sweet honey. What would she give for something a little bit savoury? Maybe a mouth-watering bite of a spicy hamburger with the tang of Spanish onions.

Exercise 1

tempting, juicy, delicate, sugarless

Exercise 2

delicious prawns; tasteless bread; hot (spicy) chicken; stale cake; minty sauce; sour milk

Exercise 3

sweet, bitter, mouth-watering

Exercise 4

chilly peppers – spicy, hot; watery cordial – weak, tasteless; baked chicken – tender, scrumptious

Word study 1

unripe – green, immature; bitter – sharp, sour; appetising – mouth watering, delectable; sample – taste, try

Word study 2

aftertaste – a taste that lingers in the mouth; taste buds – (elevated) parts of the tongue where taste sensations are experienced; flat – without effervescence (bubbles); sweet tooth – strong liking for sweet foods

Exercise 5

pecking – chickens; lapping – dogs; gnawing – rats

Research

The experience was unpleasant/ disappointing or caused regret.

Exercise 6

sweet, sickly, gooey, scrumptious, iced

17 Creating characters Page 63

Exercise 1

Harry Potter: quiet, loyal, honest, clever; Bugs Bunny: cheeky, lively, daring

Exercise 3

1. hobble – old man; stagger – very ill person; dawdle – tired student; sneak – thief; stumble – tired runner; hurry – school teacher who is late for class
2. ordered – sergeant; pleaded – prisoner; mumbled – grumpy child; demanded – bully; whined – spoilt child; stuttered – frightened offender
3. peep – cheat; stare – sports spectator; gape – astonished person; spy – sneaky person; study – tourist; glance – teacher

Exercise 4

Checklist points	Male character	Female character
Physical appearance	lanky	tall
Movements	slovenly	determined
Behaviour to others	rude	respectful
Dialogue	indistinct	snappy
Physical environment	mining town	beach suburb
Character's past	skipped class	sport success
Name	Dan	Cassandra

Exercise 5

fast food outlet – male, teenager; ballet-goer – female, middle aged; life saver – male, early twenties

18 Giving characters names Page 67

Exercise 1

Edward, Elsie, Wilma, Theodore, May, Doreen

Exercise 2

Shorty; Bing, Whacka, Bugsy

Exercise 3

Older males: Wilfred, Henry, Mervyn; Older females: Edith, Gertrude, Sheila; Younger people: Tracy-Anne, Sean; Mischievous children: Dennis, Matilda, Lorenzo; Unusual characters: Holly, Lofty, Elfin, Xavier

Exercise 4

1. Peter Streeter, Jane Lane, Fay May, Hugh Blue
2. Barry Brown, Wendy Wilson, Robin Rose

19 Giving characters real character Page 70

Exercise 2

bold – speaks loudly; lazy – leaves clothes on the floor; thoughtful – does chores without being told; cheerful – smiles often; selfish – takes the largest piece of pizza; clumsy – trips over things; disorganised – forgets where he/she left things; restless – walks around the room often

Exercise 3

1. considerate; 2. suspicious, upset, agitated, annoyed

Exercise 4

1. 'I can't do that,' groaned Alvin. 'I can't do that,' giggled Alvin. 'I can't do that,' gasped Alvin. 'I can't do that,' sighed Alvin.
2. 'What are you doing here?' demanded the school teacher. 'What are you doing here?' inquired her best friend. 'What are you doing here?' beamed my mother as she came into my room. 'What are you doing here?' hissed the swimming coach.

20 Showing, not telling Page 74

Exercise 1

Most people would agree passage 1 is better story writing. It lets the reader use his/her imagination and experiences. The reader is not told everything. The reader's interest is aroused and he/she will want to read on.

Exercise 2

(possible interpretations)

1. trying to stop the car from rolling, possible onset of unexpected pain
2. feeling sick, pills, rough
3. scared/cold

Exercise 3

1. He pulled his collar up around his neck.
2. He wet his lips with his tongue.
3. She headed straight for the teacher's desk.
4. He dropped his coat on the armchair.
5. I could feel my ears going red.
6. His smile showed a full set of perfect teeth.
7. He leaned back in his chair and smiled.
8. She looked at it for several seconds and then nodded.

Exercise 4

1. He stopped abruptly and his shoulders sagged.
2. 'Well, well, well,' he said to himself.
3. He dropped his bag and gave a long, loud whistle.
4. The smile on his face turned to a frown.

Reading and writing task

1. evening; 2. fishing; 3. concern; 4. felt guilty; 5. ants; 6. confused

Reading task 2

1. no; 2. isolated situation; 3. campers, workers

21 Selecting a point of view Page 78

Student responses

22 Finding other words for 'said' Page 81

Exercise 1

1. 'Turn that motor off now!' ordered the foreman.

2. 'Oh, I hope that's not more bad news,' sighed the upset mother.
3. 'I will pay you a million dollars for that shirt,' joked my father.
4. 'But you aren't listening to my complaint,' protested the customer.
5. 'Give it back!' snapped the new student.

Exercise 2

'Your truck should be moved off the footpath,' Bill suggested.

'You now owe me one hundred dollars,' Dad joked.

Word study

preach – to promote a virtue or truth; rant – to speak loudly or violently; state – to declare something with confidence; claim – to say something is fact; confirm – to support a particular thing that has been said; chide – to pester someone into action

Writing task

'Do you think we are lost?' snarled Peter looking at the broken sign.

'I hope not,' moaned Penny, shaking her head.

'Let me see the compass. Maybe you got it wrong,' accused Peter angrily.

'But I only did it the way you told me,' objected Penny, glaring at him.

23 Finding other words for 'look'

Page 85

Exercise 1

1. Mr Rufus glared at the class over his half frame glasses.
2. The detective spied a small brooch in the dying grass.
3. Jake peered at the small print on the menu in the dim cafe.
4. Dr Jackson observed the behaviour of the rats in their cages.
5. Kerry had a quick peek at the book on her mother's desk.

Exercise 2

Examining something small (looking for clues)

Word study

scan – a quick read of information; scowl – to look in a threatening/angry manner; gape – to stare in wonder; bird's eye view – as seen from high above; behold – to look at/observe; watch tower – high structure for a sentry's post

Exercise 4

1. The driver studied the track, which was being covered with floodwater.
2. The driver glared at the track, which was being covered with floodwater.
3. The driver gaped at the track, which was being covered with floodwater.
4. The driver scanned the track, which was being covered with floodwater.
5. The driver recognised the track, which was being covered with floodwater.

Reading task 3

Peter and his sister, Gail, stood outside the toyshop window. They gazed in wonder at the colourful display. Surveying the toys available, Peter wondered what he might get for Christmas. Then he spied a multi-coloured space ship. He could picture the machine sitting on his homework desk.

Gail eyed a book with pop-up pictures. It was open at the middle page and she could make out goblins sitting under giant toadstools. They had large saucer-like eyes that seemed to stare out at her.

Neither child suspected that they were being quietly observed by their father.

Exercise 5

1. examining; 2. sighting; 3. searching; 4. witnessing; 5. peering

Research

1. glare a warning; 2. being a 'sticky-beak'/ ill-mannered staring; 3. look down in shame

24 Finding other words for 'went'

Page 89

Exercise 1

1. Our dog, Scruffy, bounded across the park to greet my sister.
2. The scouts paddled across the shallow lake to the campsite.
3. The small birds flitted from one flower to the next.
4. Simone rented a canoe and rowed across

the bay.
5. The class, hot and weary, struggled all the way to the oval.

Exercise 2

dribbling

Word study

trundle – to move heavily (as if on wheels); ramble – to stroll about freely; twirl – to move around rapidly in circles; file – to walk in a (single) line; thread – to make one's way through/over something; rolling stone – wandering restless person

Exercise 4

1. The pirate hobbled along the wharf until he found his boat.
2. The pirate sneaked along the wharf until he found his boat.
3. The pirate strutted along the wharf until he found his boat.
4. The pirate slunk along the wharf until he found his boat.
5. The pirate scurried along the wharf until he found his boat.

Reading task 3

Mr Joseph hurried from the store. He was late for his appointment and he'd have to run to the bus stop. He skipped around a lady wheeling a pram and dodged past a courier slipping out of a doorway.

Then he stumbled.

Ignoring the looks of bystanders, he crawled quickly to his feet and limped to the bus stop, only to see the bus chugging into the streaming traffic.

He turned around and hobbled off to find a taxi.

Exercise 5

1. slink; 2. prowl; 3. dashing; 4. tip-toeing; 5. darting

Research

1. run uncontrollably; 2. haphazard or careless movements; 3. walk dejectedly

25 Structuring a story Page 93

Exercise 1

Beginning: Girl walks through woods to take gift to grandmother's home.

Problem: Girl meets wolf.

Complications: Girl tells wolf where she is going; wolf plans to hurry ahead to Grandma's cottage and eat her and then the girl.

Climax: Wolf tricks girl into thinking that he is Grandma.

Resolution: Woodman saves girl and dispenses with wolf.

Exercise 2

Hare brags he is fastest runner. Challenges all animals to race. Tortoise accepts much to hare's mirth. Race begins. Hare is so sure of himself he has a sleep along the way. Tortoise passes hare and wins.

Reading task

Lion and the Mouse; Town Mouse and Country Mouse; Ant and the Grasshopper

Writing task

Jack has to sell his poor mother's cow. Jack exchanges the cow for bean seeds. Overnight the beans grow to the sky. Jack climbs the beanstalk and enters the bad giant's castle. Jack takes the giant's possessions. He is nearly caught by the giant but manages to escape down the beanstalk. He chops the beanstalk down and kills the giant. Jack and his mother are no longer poor.

26 Using metaphors, similes and clichés Page 97

Exercise 1

Although the blossoms were as red as blood now, by nightfall they would be like used bandages. Craig wondered if he should have bought plastic flowers. At least they didn't curl up and wilt like fairy floss in the hot sun. Trouble was they looked as phoney as the set of a school play.

Exercise 2

Joan's bedroom was a pigsty. In the far corner was a pile of dirty clothes waiting to do battle with any individual who might even consider removing them to the laundry. The hastily discarded school exercise books made a variety of badly built pyramids on her desk.

Exercise 3

1. Every big city is no more than a jungle.
2. One of the twins was a lion, the other was a lamb.
3. The golden path to happiness is difficult to find.

Reading task

He entered the room that was as dark as a crypt on a winter's night.

Writing task

Gwen took the letter from the letterbox as if it were on fire.

Gwen took the letter from the letterbox as if it were a smelly rag.

Gwen took the letter from the letterbox as if it were as fragile as a crystal glass.

Exercise 4

Dead branches, like the arms of drowning swimmers reached for the sky. Growth abnormalities on the trunks looked like giant warts. Ancient bushfire burns reminded Shane of oil stains on a garage floor.

Exercise 5

1. The helicopter hovered like a dragonfly.
2. The locomotive roared through the night like an angry dragon.
3. The space station watched the earth below like a silent bird of prey.

Extension exercise 1

clouds, in the sky

27 Using different text types Page 101

Exercise 1

has a university education, has knowledge of old model computers, runs a small business

Exercise 3

it looks like fun; there are lots of things to do; it might be cheap; some of the sideshows might be 'fakes'

Research

1. Witch/wizard card; 2. School posters

28 Looking at the features of a story Page 104

1. Oops, wrong choice!
2. a notice
3. a very delicate scent
4. Harley and his father were spiked by the cactus.
5. bounced into the air like a football
6. makes reader wonder what the wrong choice is
7. last line is 'opposite' of the title
8. declared, shouted, agreed
9. happy, full of enthusiasm, organiser
10. 'Great idea,' declared Dad./Quickly organises to get plants
11. quiet, calm, thoughtful
12. smiling/ not upset by her father's opinion
13. students' individual responses (Jasmine is the name of a scented flower)
14. earthenware tub/canvas chair
15. And I smiled.
16. Jasmine